Flexible Access to Vocational Qualifications

Second Edition, Revised and Updated

John Pursaill and Mary Potter

NIACE
THE NATIONAL ORGANISATION
FOR ADULT LEARNING

Published by the National Institute of Adult Continuing Education
(England and Wales)
21 De Montfort Street, Leicester LE1 7GE
Company registration no. 2603322
Charity registration no. 1002775

First published 1994

Cataloguing in Publication Data
A CIP record for this title is available from the British Library

ISBN 1 872941 52 4

Printed and bound in Great Britain by
Biddles Ltd, Guildford and King's Lynn

CONTENTS

Chapter 4: COLLEGE CASE STUDIES

FOREWORD

Since the first edition of this book appeared four years ago, there has been a massive growth of recognition that the UK's future prosperity depends on its population becoming more skilful, more knowledgeable and more responsive to change than it has hitherto been. The need to extend the learning community to more and different groups of adults is recognised by the National Targets for Education and Training, endorsed by government, business and trade unions. NIACE, the national organisation for adult learning, has also welcomed the targets as having an important part to play in the creation of a learning society with mass adult participation in education and training. In these circumstances it is to be hoped that such an aim is neither diluted nor fudged in the current review of the targets but rather extended to include those currently unemployed and unwaged. It will be another missed opportunity if attention is once more focused on improving the skill levels of those already qualified rather than the more demanding task of realising the potential of those groups which, traditionally, have benefited least from schooling or from training.

The qualification framework described in the first edition has also changed considerably. National Vocational Qualifications are now largely in place and are being complemented by the introduction of General National Vocational Qualifications (GNVQs). NVQs are not without their critics – and there is certainly a case for reviewing the necessary linkage between competence and underpinning knowledge. Similarly, GNVQs, which were designed primarily with new entrants to the labour market in mind, are something of an unknown when it comes to meeting the aspirations of adult learners.

The foreword to the first edition of *Flexible Access* noted that vocational qualifications are most accessible to young people in initial training and to adults in full-time work. Since then, the size of the so-called 'flexible workforce' has grown, according to Employment Department figures, to more than 35 per cent of those in employment. Even if narrower definitions are taken, the challenge remains to make access to VQs easier by changing the ways in which the costs of learning and assessment are expressed;

by organising teaching and learning in new ways and by removing rules and regulations which result from unnecessary, outdated or self-interested practices within the education and training system.

The original report was funded by REPLAN, the Department of Education and Science/Welsh Office programme to promote the development of learning opportunities for unemployed adults. Although that programme came to an end in 1991, the need for it did not, and it is particularly welcome that the new edition retains a concern to ensure that the needs of unwaged and unemployed learners are a prime concern.

NIACE is grateful to those colleges which agreed to act as case studies. Whilst two of the case studies are of institutions not featured in the first edition, the remaining three will provide readers who have access to the earlier edition with an opportunity to assess the extent of the considerable changes in the intervening period, which also covers the colleges' move from local education authority institutions to becoming independent corporations. Having directed the project which led to the original report, I am also pleased to acknowledge, once again, our thanks to John Pursaill and his co-author Mary Potter for providing an updated snapshot of current issues and practice.

Alastair Thomson
Planning and Development Officer, NIACE

CHAPTER 1

Context and Purpose

EDUCATION AND TRAINING TARGETS AND ADULTS

Education and training for adults has become a national priority. Forecasts suggest that, despite current levels of unemployment, there will not be enough qualified young people to meet industry's need for new workers over the next decade. Even were that not so, the need for a better trained workforce is too pressing to wait for initial training of young people to effect this.

National education and training targets, overseen by the National Advisory Council for Education and Training Targets (NACETT), reflect the need for a future workforce that has a much greater proportion of highly qualified people. They include the following 'lifetime learning' targets for 1996:

- at least half the employed workforce should be aiming for NVQ qualifications or units towards them
- at least half the workforce should be qualified to NVQ level 3 or equivalent.

As regards new entrants to the workforce, the CBI has commented:

There are three groups to whom employers may look to meet their skill requirements: women returners, given that women are predicted to provide 90 per cent of the workforce increase over the next decade; older workers, whose numbers will grow significantly over the next ten years; the long-term unemployed. (Towards a Skills Revolution, CBI, October 1989.)

While current 'lifetime' targets relate only to the employed, there is growing pressure for NACETT to define targets that include the unemployed (see 'Tackling Targets' in the Further Education Unit's April 1994 *Newsletter*, which also outlines FEU projects and reports in this area). More specific local targets are set by a strategic forum established by each Training and Enterprise Council with members from industry and education, whose role is to agree strategies for achieving targets and to co-ordinate their implementation. It is important for colleges to identify their own

1

targets and be active in the local Forum and its committees – all the more so since Further Education Funding Council funding is closely aligned to National Targets.

THREATS AND OPPORTUNITIES FOR FURTHER EDUCATION

There are a number of reasons why adults have come to be recognised as a more crucial target group for FE than ever before:

- FEFC funding requires colleges to increase student numbers by 25 per cent by 1995
- there is growing competition from schools offering GNVQs to full-time students at age 16 and above – this is likely to increase radically over the next few years
- colleges are now wholly self-managed and depend on output-related funding in a way they did not before
- the NVQ framework is now largely in place and has been extended by GNVQs – their unit base and 'outcome' form makes it possible to reduce many barriers to adult access
- FEFC outcomes funding much reduces and may remove differences between full-time (mostly 16–18) and part-time (mostly adult) students
- FEFC has now approved programmes accredited by Open College Networks as evidence for progression and basic education,[1] and open college credits can now count towards Foundation and Lifetime Targets[2]
- adults represent a much greater (and largely untapped) potential market for education and training than young people and, where access is significantly improved, there is clear evidence that numbers can rise quickly and dramatically.

The NVQ framework is designed to open access to vocational qualifications for students of all kinds. Adults already form over half the FE population and, in some colleges, much more than this. Yet unemployed and unwaged adults are still poorly represented

---

1 Under Schedule 2 – *Guidance on Funding Methodology 1994–5*, FEFC December 1993 (paragraph 49 v and vii)
2 Agreement between National Open College Network and the Employment Department

and many college systems remain geared, to a large extent, to full-time courses for young people. Under the new system the needs of adults and young people can be linked. There is the opportunity to meet both kinds of need within a single framework rather than by separate and very different types of programme. Staff in colleges and teams responding to new demands find that:

- the approach called for in NVQ programmes for young people leads to flexible delivery methods that can increase adult access
- there is spin-off for young people from the focus on individual need and achievement required to improve access for unwaged adults.

THE SCALE OF CHANGE

In 1989 a Further Education Unit publication *(Implications for Competence-Based Curricula)* contained the following prediction:

The most striking features, then [of a system based on vocational competence and NVQs], for the FE system as a whole relate to the breadth and depth of the change which will be required. The number of staff who will be directly affected over the next three or four years will be greater than for the advent of the Business and Technician Education Council (BTEC), the Youth Training Scheme (YTS), and the Certificate of Pre-Vocational Education (CPVE) combined.

The full effect of these changes has still to be felt. However, the growing range of occupational NVQs at levels 1–4, introduction of general NVQs (GNVQs) across some 15 sectors by 1995/96, and the need for assessor training to Training and Development Lead Body (TDLB) standards, mean that most FE staff will be directly involved in the new system by that date. In many colleges and for many staff the process is now well advanced and involves:

- more flexible programme delivery, including open learning, modular and resource-based approaches
- an increased role in workplace assessment and in meeting training needs of both individual clients and employers – in many cases closer involvement with industry if colleges are to play a real part in NVQs

3

- sharper focus on learner services such as entry guidance and diagnosis, APL (as defined by NCVQ) and assessment on demand, independent learning materials and personal tutor support, individual action-planning coupled with regular progress reviews and detailed records of achievement
- active marketing involving new kinds of work and aimed at new clients
- a major shift of staff and resources towards these activities, and new resourcing systems to meet new priorities
- college structures, job descriptions and staff skills that support these changes.

RESOURCING NEW SERVICES

Until now, teacher 'contact' and FTE-based costing systems have often made it difficult for colleges to compete with private sector bodies on equal terms. College funding has not been suited to a system based on outcomes, quick response and flexible delivery – it has made it hard to meet new client needs and to shift resources to new college functions not related to traditional classes and notions of 'bums on seats'.

Colleges now have much greater freedom to use and allocate resources. New funding criteria call for greater emphasis on access, growth, retention of students and thus quality of provision, linked with new staff conditions of service. In addition, by 1996 Training Credits will extend to all 16- and 17-year-olds leaving full-time education and training, and will be tied to NVQs wherever possible (see FEU Bulletin of January 1993, *Training Credits: The implications for colleges*). This is likely to increase demand for flexible programmes – all the more if, as has been mooted, training credits are extended to adults. These changes should make it both easier and more urgent to:

- direct funds to services needed to attract and provide for a wider range of vocational clients
- apply indicators that support response to client and community needs, by taking account of outcomes and achievement as well as inputs.

4

DRAWING ON EXPERIENCE

Through the 1980s further education became increasingly involved in work with unwaged adults. Earlier MSC and Department of Employment initiatives and, since 1988, Employment Training (ET), Adult Training and now Training for Work (TFW) have led to varied and often imaginative provision. From 1984 to 1991 many colleges worked with NIACE or FEU on projects under the REPLAN programme, and many more linked with NIACE REPLAN field staff in seeking ways to meet the needs of a wider range of unwaged clients. More recently some colleges have opened access for non-employed adults and other mature students to a growing range of NVQs, and now GNVQs.

Much has been learned. Within colleges growing experience and expertise has led to new kinds of provision and new levels of institutional response. Local networks for the unwaged have been set up in many areas: LEAs, education guidance services, government agencies, voluntary bodies, community groups and others have worked with colleges to reach the unwaged in their communities, remove barriers to access and provide the guidance and support needed to increase participation in further education. Colleges are also increasingly working with local employers, TECs and other training bodies in schemes that gear provision to the needs of local industry and the local job market.

However, experience of 'access' provision and flexible delivery may lie in separate sections of the college and may not always be seen as part of the 'further education mainstream'. In many colleges there are likely to be a number of different strands that need to be drawn together as a basis for further development, which may include:

- experience of unwaged and other adult needs through 'access' courses
- 'outreach' activity based on adult or community education departments, often linked with a local Education Guidance Service for Adults
- what used to be called '21 hour' courses, ET and their successors
- flexible and modular approaches used in these and other programmes, e.g. YT/YTS, special courses for companies, NVQs and GNVQs

5

- work and experience in action-planning and APL, guidance systems, open learning, credit accumulation, workplace assessment and industry liaison – whether for NVQs or other programmes
- work with OCNs and on OCN-accredited courses, especially but not only where this includes vocational provision for adults
- experience in diagnosing and developing core skills, especially with adults
- up-to-date knowledge of local firms from college-industry training schemes and work placements for full-time students.

In 1989 NIACE REPLAN published with the Employment Department's Training Agency *Further Education and Employment Training: A quality response.* This provided an audit checklist for systematic review of adult education and training initiatives, including staff experience and delivery methods, college resources and local networks. In particular, it offered a method for colleges to:

- identify existing relevant experience
- identify suitable staff and resources
- identify gaps in expertise
- plan a strategic response.

Of even greater value to colleges is the 1992 FEU –NIACE joint publication: *Quality Education for the Adult Unemployed: A manual for planners and managers in further education.* It deals with strategic planning, marketing, curriculum and operational management, and provides planning charts, checklists of key issues, and illustrative case studies for those seeking to adopt a systematic approach at institutional level.

NIACE AND REPLAN

Between 1984 and 1991 more than 100 projects to promote the educational opportunities of unwaged adults were sponsored under the REPLAN programme. They offer a wealth of experience and detailed findings on, for example:

- the needs of different groups amongst the unwaged
- ways in which colleges have sought to overcome barriers to access and meet education and training needs

- curriculum design and delivery methods applied to specific groups and courses
- curriculum models and checklists for action.

It is not the purpose of this handbook to summarise these projects. This was done fully in *Drawing on Experience: REPLAN projects review* (NIACE and FEU, 1990), which draws on the whole experience of both NIACE and FEU REPLAN programmes. Those concerned to attract adult clients are strongly advised to study this review and, through it, to obtain other project reports which will be of value in their work. Of particular interest also is the report of an Employment Department-sponsored enquiry into adult learners in colleges of further education, *Opening Colleges to Adult Learners* (edited by Veronica McGivney, NIACE, 1991).

PURPOSE OF THE HANDBOOK

Few projects have focused directly on vocational certification for the unwaged. While opportunities for unit credit in vocational education and training have grown considerably since the first edition of this handbook (1990), they have so far been realised perhaps less than might have been expected. The purpose of this publication is to:

- outline opportunities for improving access to vocational certification under the emerging qualification framework
- illustrate modular and flexible delivery methods and put forward suggested approaches
- relate these approaches to the needs of adult unwaged and other students, and to learner services designed to meet such needs
- provide examples of college strategies for open access and flexible delivery.

While drawing attention to needs of the adult unwaged the report also raises some more general issues faced by colleges and staff teams as they adapt to the demands of a new system. Chapter 2 overviews the new framework for vocational qualifications, details main elements and raises issues on access and credit accumulation. Chapter 3 illustrates flexible delivery methods and issues that arise in their use by drawing on developing practice in a range of vocational areas. In Chapter 4, five college case studies show a range of strategies for planned change towards an open access and learner-centred system.

CHAPTER 2
A New Framework For Access

THE NVQ FRAMEWORK

The NVQ framework is now largely in place and will increasingly offer improved opportunities for access to vocational qualifications. These opportunities and related issues are outlined later in this chapter. However, recent developments make it important first to review the current position for both occupational NVQs and the newly introduced GNVQs.

NATIONAL VOCATIONAL QUALIFICATIONS

There has been considerable development in the coverage and form of NVQs in the past few years, including improvements in access. The main aspects of this are outlined below.

Overall coverage

Although gaps remain both in certain occupational areas and for higher and professional levels, NVQs now exist at levels 1–3 and often 1–4 for the main vocational areas and, in one or two cases, have already been accredited at level 5. 'Conditional' NVQs (those that did not fully meet NCVQ criteria, perhaps because they were not unit-based and/or offered limited access in other ways) have now been replaced and NCVQ has published a substantial *Guide to National Vocational Qualifications*. This is regularly updated and sets out NVQ design criteria that include access to assessment, credit accumulation and equal opportunities.

Choice of NVQ awarding body

While in some occupational areas there is only one awarding body, for many NVQs there are now three or more bodies each separately accredited to approve centres, provide for assessment and issue certificates. In such cases those offering NVQs can choose which body to work with. This tends to make for improved access and wider variety in the structure of provision, for lower charges and for fee structures that support acquisition of individual units as well as full NVQs.

Broader concept of competence

Early NVQs were often based on a narrow concept of competence and focused on limited work tasks and skills at the expense of broader competences. A number of steps have been taken to counteract this:

- industry lead bodies have adopted 'functional analysis' in developing the national standards used for NVQs; this means that NVQ units and the 'elements' they comprise are related to broad occupational functions rather than narrow job tasks
- 'range statements' have been introduced to define a range of different situations and contexts in which each competence is to be applied
- use of 'common units' is encouraged – these may be common to NVQs in a given occupational area (e.g. Health and Social Care), to NVQs in related areas (e.g. Business Administration and related areas such as Banking, Accounting, etc.), or to NVQs in any area (e.g. units designed for NVQs in Management are used for level 3 and 4 awards in many areas)
- NCVQ has designed 'core skill' units at five levels which can now be awarded independently of other programmes (see below under GNVQs), and is encouraging their use with NVQs.

NVQs and FE colleges

The following points should be borne in mind when considering access to NVQs through FE colleges:

(a) NVQs are designed to be industry-based and some do not involve FE, while others (e.g. Retail) are available only through specialist colleges

(b) within main vocational areas the range of NVQs offered depends on local demand and financial viability, industry links and expertise at the particular college

(c) many NVQs have only recently been accredited to awarding bodies, assessment systems are not yet always in place and, in a number of cases, it may be some time before many colleges are in a position to deliver them

(d) new areas are continually coming on stream, and it is important to keep in touch with these through the *NVQ Monitor* published by NCVQ

(e)   many colleges now have significant involvement in a wide
      range of areas, either as main providers and/or as partners
      with industry. These may include for example:
      Administration, Agriculture, Construction, Catering and
      Hospitality, Design, Hairdressing and Beauty Therapy,
      Health and Social Care, Management, Sport and
      Recreation, Travel Services.

GENERAL NATIONAL VOCATIONAL QUALIFICATIONS

GNVQs have the potential to offer greatly improved access to
vocational qualifications for a wide range of people, including the
non-employed. Their main features, introduction and impact are
outlined below.

Main features

GNVQs are intended to provide a broad base of knowledge,
understanding and skills for a range of careers and are designed
to be delivered in colleges and schools. They are unit-based and
share other NVQ features, with the following main differences:

- units are made up of 'Elements of Achievement' rather than
  'Elements of Competence'
- although assessment is primarily through evidence of
  performance, there are end of unit tests to check basic
  'underpinning knowledge'
- overall performance (not individual units) is graded 'pass',
  'merit', or 'distinction', using criteria that focus on learner
  autonomy and skills in planning, information handling and
  evaluation
- work experience, though valuable, is not a required element
  for GNVQs
- 'core skills' (especially those in Communication, Application
  of Number and IT) are central to provision, with units in
  these an integral feature of each award.

Programme for introduction

BTEC, City and Guilds and RSA are currently accredited to award
GNVQs, which will ultimately be offered at NVQ levels 1–4 (and
perhaps 5) in about 15 vocational areas. In 'Phase 1' (from
September 1992) some 100 centres, each approved by one of the
three awarding bodies, introduced programmes for level 2

(Intermediate) and 3 (Advanced) GNVQs in Art and Design, Business, Health and Social Care, Leisure and Tourism and Manufacturing. These titles were generally available to approved colleges and schools from September 1993, when Built Environment, Hospitality and Catering and Science were piloted by selected centres at Intermediate and Advanced levels, with Foundation (level 1) GNVQs in all five 'Phase 1' vocational areas.

Distribution, Engineering, Information Technology, Management (Advanced level only), and Media and Communication will be piloted from September 1994, with Land Based Industries following in 1995. By 1995/96 a full range of GNVQs at levels 1–3 will be generally available to schools and colleges. While there are plans for level 4 GNVQs, work on these has yet to begin.

Flexibility of GNVQs

GNVQs are extremely flexible, bridge the 'academic/vocational divide' and provide a route to higher and further education as well as to employment and occupational NVQs. Their flexibility stems from a choice of more specialised 'option' as well as 'mandatory' units, and from the fact that they may be extended by other studies to suit individual learner needs. Such studies may comprise, for example:

- 'additional' GNVQ vocational units provided by Awarding Bodies
- foreign language units provided by the Languages Lead Body and accredited by NCVQ
- units from appropriate NVQs
- GCSEs and A/AS-levels, or other learning.

At the same time, GNVQs may be attained by any mode of attendance over any period, whether shorter or longer than a 'normal' programme, depending on individual student needs and centre/college provision. Programme flexibility is likely to be further increased as a result of SCAA guidelines which allow for 'modular' A-levels with modules of similar size to GNVQ units.

GNVQs and core skills

A further important feature of GNVQs is their strong focus on core skills – communication, application of number, information technology skills, self-evaluation – as a basis for personal development and progression. Core skills are assessed through specific units, may be attained at a variety of levels, are developed through work on GNVQ vocational units and are strongly supported by the criteria used for grading. These units may be awarded separately, and are being used by some colleges to provide the basis for initial access, return to work and return to study programmes, often accredited by OCNs.

Phasing out of other vocational awards

At present other vocational awards (e.g. BTEC Firsts and Nationals, RSA certificates, City and Guilds Diploma of Vocational Education) may be run alongside GNVQs. This will continue for a transitional period which differs for vocational areas depending on when GNVQs were first introduced, and is likely to vary between colleges. By 1996/97 GNVQs will have replaced most other general vocational awards offered full-time for levels 1–3, although Awarding Bodies are likely to retain some awards that meet needs not clearly met by GNVQs. The position for part-time programmes and qualifications is less clear: GNVQs may demand more study time than a typical part-time programme can easily provide, and other qualifications may continue for a longer period.

ACCESS AND THE NVQ FRAMEWORK

Access to awards is a high priority of the NVQ/GNVQ system and improved access to certification one of the main criteria applied when NCVQ accredits Awarding Bodies. Main features of the system for both NVQs and GNVQs are outlined below with special reference to access.

Competence base

NVQ and GNVQ units are written in the language of outcomes related to employment, and a unit/outcomes approach is increasingly being adopted for other programmes such as those accredited by OCNs. Such an approach means that:

- students and tutors can see more precisely what must be achieved
- students can relate this to what they have already achieved at college, at work or through other experience

- learning programmes can be designed to build on experience in the most effective way and to exclude what is not needed by the student
- units and qualifications (including units common between awards) can be mapped against each other to extend credit and increase choice, or to develop common learning programmes and/or materials
- clearly defined outcomes make it easier to discuss needs with students and employers, plan work placements and relate programmes to what is learned at work (this applies particularly to NVQs, though work-based assessment may be included in GNVQ programmes).

Assessment

Assessment is not tied to learning programmes. It draws on evidence from past experience or achievement, from the workplace, from assignments or projects, or from any activity where relevant achievement is demonstrated. On the one hand this makes possible assessment on demand and APL and, on the other, more varied learning methods and greater flexibility in learning programmes. Students play a major role in their own assessment and can be encouraged to:

- set their own learning targets against unit/assessment specifications
- practice self-assessment, and use peer assessment at work or college, to enhance awareness of progress
- decide when they are ready to be assessed for particular competences and approach tutor or work supervisor for this
- discuss in regular reviews what needs to be learned or practised, how this can best be done, where it should be assessed and by what methods – and make action plans to implement what is agreed with tutors.

Unit credit

NVQ units generally represent discrete work functions or areas of activity. Awarding bodies should provide for separate assessment and certification for each unit and the latter should be given within a reasonable time of verified achievement (NCVQ suggests five weeks as the normal maximum period). Students should thus be able to take individual NVQ units as required and, if they wish, build them up into full awards over a period that suits them. The position for GNVQ units is similar, with two provisos:

- how far and when separate unit credit is available will depend on how the GNVQ in question is structured and delivered in a particular college
- many units include an externally set and marked test which is currently available four times a year – this must be passed before a unit certificate can be awarded.

Entry requirements

There are no formal requirements for entry to a GNVQ or NVQ programme, and students should be admitted if likely to benefit from programmes and judged able to achieve defined targets over an agreed timescale. Although some colleges still tend to determine entry by specific qualifications such as GCSEs or vocational awards, this is beginning to change as the NVQ/GNVQ system impacts more fully. Some colleges offer diagnostic or 'threshold' programmes of 5–10 weeks that allow vocational work to be assessed at two or more levels, so that the right target NVQ/GNVQ level is identified for each student. Many now have open access policies and assess potential through interviews, records of achievement, diagnostic tests and student motivation: 'we rarely if ever reject a student – decisions to withdraw or enter at a different level are made by students themselves after counselling and diagnosis'.

NVQ database

The database gives details of all vocational qualifications and includes units, elements of achievement/competence, performance criteria and range statements for NVQs and GNVQs. Launched in May 1990, the database is available on subscription for industry-standard personal computers. Its latest version includes facilities for (a) 'Local Notes' (e.g. on programmes and learning materials for each qualification and unit, or on other related college provision) and (b) individual student action-planning and records of achievement covering each unit and element. This enables colleges and others to develop databanks that can be used:

- by staff teams to map the content of awards and design programmes that take account of common elements

15

- by college management to record routes, programmes, services and materials, assessment methods and requirements, staff and staff time available for each award and unit
- by learners and staff to identify prior achievement, to select awards and learning routes/methods, and to make action plans and record achievement for each unit they are taking
- by employers and other clients to identify needs and ways of meeting them.

Some colleges have decided to enter all their provision in a databank – including college-based modules or units designed for particular needs and client groups, as back-up and support, or as bridging units for entry to other programmes. As the database becomes more accessible, e.g. through TAPs, Education Guidance Services for Adults and industry-linked centres, it should prove a major aid in marketing college programmes to adults.

BARRIERS TO ACCESS

Much has been done by NCVQ and others in recent years to remove barriers to access and credit accumulation. Some problems which have been common are outlined below. Although these have been dealt with in many cases, there are still occasions where they may arise and it is important for those concerned to take them up with relevant awarding bodies.

Equal opportunities

All bodies accredited to award NVQs/GNVQs are required to have an effective equal opportunities policy and to see that this is implemented by centres offering awards. Thus, for example, where students have disabilities that affect their ability to undergo written tests, alternative means must be found to assess them.

Unit certificates not available

Certificates may be available for one or more units but not generally given until the programme has been completed by a cohort of students. Unit certificates should now be available at any point and within a reasonable time from notification to awarding bodies that unit(s) has been achieved. Problems have sometimes arisen because an awarding body has not been used to issuing certificates for individual units. However, such problems are more likely to arise from college practice in notifying results to awarding bodies.

High charge for unit certificates

Individual units may be certified but fees for single units may be excessive. Awarding body practice varies and administrative costs for individual certificates need to be covered. However, some bodies have special pricing structures geared to those wishing to obtain unit-based rather than full NVQ certificates. NCVQ accreditation criteria include a requirement that unit certificate charges should not be excessive.

Location and cost of assessment

For some NVQs assessment is by competence tests which may involve (a) a long journey to the test centre; (b) a test which may last two or three days; (c) fees high enough to exclude those not paid for by their employer. This can apply particularly in Construction.

Timing of assessment

Where external assessment is used (e.g. written tests to check underpinning knowledge) this may be held only at certain times of the year and entail a wait for those completing units at some point beforehand. However, in most cases awarding bodies now make such tests available at regular points through the year (e.g. monthly). GNVQs are at present an exception, with tests provided four times a year.

Workplace-only assessment

In some sectors workplace assessment may tend to be seen as the only acceptable method, thus denying access to those not employed and/or who cannot obtain suitable work placement – this currently applies, for example, in Health and Social Care and Retail. In other areas (e.g. Catering and Hospitality) the concept of 'realistic work environment' has been introduced to allow assessment in college-based facilities. By contrast, some workplace assessment is now required in (Business) Administration which in the past was often assessed entirely through simulation. However, such assessment may be carried out in college-based commercial offices.

17

Industry-based NVQs and college provision

A related problem concerns NVQs based in industry rather than colleges. While a college may decide to offer available NVQs only in certain areas there are some which are almost exclusively offered through industry-based centres, and colleges are involved, if at all, in programmes for 'underpinning knowledge' and not in training or assessing for competence. In these cases the non-employed can obtain NVQs only if the college can arrange work placement and assessment at an industry-based NVQ centre (e.g. Health and Social Care and Retail). However, many colleges are now partners in industry–education consortia accredited for Care sector NVQs, and frequently take the leading role in such partnerships. This is likely to increase their ability to offer work placement and workplace assessment to college-based students.

Training programme requirement

Access to an award may depend on (a) completing a given training programme (for which there may be high fees); (b) attending a given course where a minimum time element is attached either to the course or to individual units. This restricts access to those who can and are prepared to attend the whole programme, whatever their level of competence. Although NCVQ strongly discourages such practice it can still be the norm in some sectors (e.g. Engineering), where it may prove difficult for clients to obtain NVQs by other routes.

Time-serving in a job

The rules of a professional or other body may require a period of employment (e.g. 18 months) in a given type of job for those seeking professional status. Although such rules affected some NVQs in the past, this no longer applies – the NVQ should be distinct from professional status and access should not be affected by the rule.

Verification

Systems for awarding and assessing NVQs must be verified by an outside person approved for this (External Verifier). Access is affected where visits are not frequent if the verifier must (a) view or sample student achievement or (b) scrutinise pass lists – *before* a unit certificate is given. Although this has applied to many NVQs it is now usually the role of an Internal Verifier (e.g. designated member of college staff) to verify individual results while the External Verifier reviews the assessment system as a whole. Unit certificates can thus be sought as soon as achievement has been internally verified.

Registration requirements

Candidates may be required to register for an award or unit: (a) at a specified time (e.g. 12 weeks) 'after the beginning of the course'; (b) a specified time before an assessment. While requirement (a) is not generally specified by awarding bodies, it may be normal practice within a college. Awarding bodies vary as regards (b), some requiring three months' notice prior to assessment while others will accept previous assessment once a student has registered and achievement is verified.

REMOVING BARRIERS

Changing practice

There are other barriers that relate to costs and funding, and to college implementation of NVQ and GNVQ programmes: students may be faced with high fees for programmes or assessment and may have problems obtaining financial support; some colleges may impose restrictive entry requirements, and/or may offer little or no opportunity for students to access individual units or to enter programmes at different stages during the year. Colleges who work with large numbers of adult and non-employed students are increasingly finding ways to avoid such barriers – these are outlined in Chapter 3 and illustrated in the case studies in Chapter 4.

As regards barriers reviewed in the previous section, awarding bodies have usually taken action to increase access. However, where this is not so, colleges are well advised to press specific questions of access with the appropriate awarding body, if necessary raising them at high levels and/or contacting NCVQ for advice.

APL and NVQs/GNVQs

All awarding bodies have accepted APL as a route to unit credit for NVQs and GNVQs, and have generally (though not always) issued guidance on its use for particular awards. While practice is still developing, it is clear that it can help remove barriers to credit accumulation. For example, where required formal or external assessment is not accessible and a student is judged to have achieved NVQ unit competences, tutors may:

- ensure that clear evidence of this is provided and that it is moderated and recorded (in sufficient detail) within internal college systems
- include this evidence in the student's record of achievement or NROA (National Record of Achievement), to be submitted for APL at a suitable stage
- support the student's application for APL by letter, detailing assessment methods and measures taken to ensure standards.

The approach can be applied to completed units or where some but not all elements have been achieved. It enables recorded credit to be carried forward and claimed from an awarding body on a subsequent occasion. However, for this to be done it will be necessary for the student to be registered at a centre approved to award the NVQ in question.

AWARDS OUTSIDE THE NVQ SYSTEM

NVQs and GNVQs will in due course replace most other vocational qualifications in FE colleges. However, during the transitional period many awards are likely to remain in their present mould and, even at the present stage, awarding bodies are still introducing some new awards outside the NVQ system. Such awards will thus continue to offer an important route to vocational certification, and access to them remains important. In particular, awards at level 4 and above (e.g. BTEC HNC/Ds, vocational degree and access programmes offered by or franchised to FE colleges, some professional qualifications) may remain outside the G/NVQ system for some time.

Unit-based qualifications

While unit-based and 'modular' approaches have become closely linked with NCVQ they also have a wider basis within FE:

- they are of value not only to unwaged adults and 'returners' but also to young people in terms of credit for achievement, increased choice and faster progression

- their use is growing for degrees, including those 'franchised' to FE colleges, for pre-degree access programmes, and for other academic qualifications
- the National Open College Network is encouraging local OCNs to promote unit/outcome-based specifications for programmes they accredit, and to provide for APL
- work is in progress to close the gap between GNVQs, the national curriculum and academic qualifications
- college-based vocational access courses are often modular or unit-based
- many vocational qualifications outside the NVQ system are modular or unit-based (e.g. all level 1–3 BTEC, many RSA and some City and Guilds awards).

Unit-based and modular schemes may not always improve access to credit accumulation – there may be barriers in the structure of awards, the design of learning programmes and their delivery. Some colleges have found ways round these barriers and have developed programmes that offer access to a range of awards, including those within and outside the NVQ system.

Awarding bodies and access policy

In recent years all major awarding bodies have improved access not only for their NVQ awards but as a matter of more general policy, for example:

- entry requirements have been relaxed for most awards
- APL is often accepted as a route to non-NVQs and guidance is issued on this
- alternative modes such as flexible learning are encouraged
- steps have been taken to increase access to unit credit. However, there may still be issues concerning: (a) charges for single units; (b) time of registration for individual units; (c) ease with which an individual unit certificate can be obtained from the awarding body.

APL and non-NVQs

It is possible for students who have worked towards but not completed a vocational qualification outside the NVQ system to carry forward their achievement towards NVQ certification. This may be of particular use where there is no relevant NVQ when the work is undertaken, and can be done whether or not the non-NVQ is unit-based, and whether or not any award component is completed or any formal assessment taken. However, it depends on detailed records of achievement, stated as far as possible in the form of clear outcomes, and authentication of supporting evidence.

Such a record can then be used later in assessing prior achievement at an approved NVQ centre. Experience suggests that a student will not gain a complete NVQ in this way and may not even be awarded a single NVQ unit. However, previous achievement will be credited and the learning programme needed to achieve G/NVQ units or awards may be sharply reduced.

CHAPTER 3

Delivering Credit

DELIVERY AND ACCESS: SOME MAJOR ISSUES

Why so few unwaged adults are at present within the FE system and how this may be tackled are matters that have been well documented.[1] There is growing evidence that very large numbers of both employed and unwaged adults are potential clients for vocational qualifications. Issues for colleges are clearly illustrated in the case study of Peterlee College (see Chapter 4), and experience suggests five major areas of action:

- making adults feel welcome at the college
- reaching them in their communities to identify needs and to let them know what programmes and services can be offered
- reducing physical and financial barriers[2] (e.g. transport, fees, time and place of provision, childcare and creches)
- tackling psychological and educational barriers by offering to each client:
  - guidance, counselling, diagnosis of need and tutor support
  - recognition of previous learning, experience and achievement
  - the chance at the outset to take tailored programmes as induction or top-up in core, learning or more specialist skills, for example
- increasing entry points and promoting flexible delivery methods.

Much has been achieved in these areas. Access to academic qualifications has been opened up on a wide scale by, for example, return to learning and 'gateway' courses, and by an increase in

---

1 See, for example: (1) *An Agenda for Access* (UDACE, January 1990); (2) *Developing Education and Training Provision for the Adult Unemployed – a Checklist* (FEU/REPLAN, 1989)
2 One in three adults left school at the minimum age and have never participated in any formal education or training since

modular and distance learning schemes based on regional open college networks. Many adults have also benefited from vocational 'access' courses. However, this work has often been outside mainstream FE vocational programmes, has tended not to affect the way in which such programmes are generally delivered and has offered 'access clients' only a limited choice of vocational qualifications.

The advent of NVQs and GNVQs has made possible a more general shift in the way vocational qualifications are delivered. Modular approaches are being applied in a growing number of vocational sectors and are increasingly linked with open and flexible learning methods. As well as enlarging vocational choice this can open up access to many who would otherwise be unlikely to be involved in FE, such as, for example, those who:

- are unwilling or unable to wait for the start of an academic year
- do not want (whether from lack of confidence or time) to commit themselves to a programme of a year or more
- have to leave a programme 'early' for domestic reasons, or to take up a job
- need formal credit after a fairly short period to boost confidence, or for a more specific purpose
- need specific units or job skills but not a whole vocational qualification, or wish to 'mix-and-match'
- want to do part of a vocational qualification and complete it at a later stage, or feel they would like to try out more than one career area and postpone final choice.

Flexible access to mainstream provision does not exclude special programmes for the unwaged – many colleges do both. Such provision has greater potential to increase the number of adults participating in FE and is the main focus of this study. However, access programmes may well remain the best way of meeting certain kinds of need and are briefly reviewed below. At the same time, vocational teams can gain much from those who work closely with unwaged adults, whether on access programmes or on adult training funded by TECs. This is confirmed by practice in case study colleges:

- sector teams are learning from 'access' tutors' experience of
  adult needs and learner-centred methods, and are making use
  of diagnostic and other services they have developed
- experience of ET and related training – e.g. problems of the
  unemployed, tailored short programmes, action planning
  with individual trainees – has been a major source of
  expertise, particularly where this involved mainstream
  programmes designed to cater for adult trainees.

'ACCESS' PROVISION

Range of access courses

Some colleges offer a wide range of vocational access courses.
Setting them up may involve outreach work and meeting local
groups in their communities to identify needs and agree on what
is to be offered. Typically, female to male ratio is high in access
groups (2:1–4:1). Types of course include:

- 'return to work' and 'access to FE' courses: may include core
  skills and personal effectiveness, job searches, CV writing
  and interview skills, vocational course and job 'tasters'
- community provision: e.g. core and basic skills and some
  NVQ units (e.g. office skills or catering), delivered in
  collaboration with voluntary groups and/or employers
- office, secretarial and IT skills: NVQs and/or RSA, PEI single
  skill certificates at different levels, clients working at their
  own pace
- professional access: e.g. preparation for police examinations,
  programmes agreed with local hospital authorities for
  entrance to student nursing
- courses for women (e.g. 'Women into Engineering'), to
  promote entry to male-dominated jobs: confidence-building,
  practical competence and skills, work experience and
  preparation for further training
- courses for those with learning difficulties or disabilities
- courses for members of ethnic communities: may provide
  support in English and community language, including the
  latter's use in business
- GNVQs: while so far offered mainly at 16-plus, programmes
  at some colleges provide for mature returners as a separate

group – there is potential for GNVQs/GNVQ units at various levels in access courses.

Often courses last a year and are scheduled between 10.00am and 3.00pm, from one to four days a week. Programmes may be shorter (e.g. 10 weeks) or in some cases 'modular', with entry each term. 'Open workshops' and flexible learning materials may be provided for language, numeracy, IT and learning skills and, sometimes, for certain vocational areas. In such cases flexible attendance and individual programmes may be offered. Much access provision includes core skill diagnostic tests and follow-up work, either as an integral part of the course or as back-up support.

Vocational certification

Opportunities for vocational certification have often been limited, especially for 'return to work' and other short courses, or for clients unable to remain on a course for the one or sometimes two years needed to complete a vocational qualification. Where unable to provide vocational awards access programmes may offer GCSEs, City and Guilds or RSA certificates in communication and other core areas, or credit through an Open College Network. In future there are likely to be wider options:

- the growing number of NVQs and GNVQs make it easier to design short access programmes (including 'tasters') that offer vocational unit credit at levels 1–3
- NCVQ's core skill units in five areas and at five levels can now be awarded independently of GNVQs; they can thus be used to provide unit credit in (for example) 'return to work' programmes and to enhance access to other programmes.

Credit through Open College Networks

Open College Networks (OCNs) plan to extend vocational credit. Much of their work has been linked with access to higher education and OCN modular schemes, credit levels and national Credit Accumulation and Transfer Agreement have been geared to this. However, there is now an increased interest in vocational work, and a growing number of local programmes deliver NVQ units and/or NCVQ core skill units. The National Open College Network is encouraging use of modular schemes based on the assessment of outcomes which, together with greater use of APL, is likely to enhance the value of OCNs to colleges and clients. The agreement with the Employment Department on including OCN credits within the data on progress towards the National Targets for Education and Training creates a formal equivalence between NVQs and OCN credits as they contribute to the national targets.

Current work on bridging the academic/vocational gap may also extend the role of OCNs. NVQs can be entered at any level, and academic study is commonly a prelude to vocational training. Programmes that include academic and vocational elements are likely to grow, supported by current work on core skills in both academic and VET circles, by APL and access to unit credit. Links could also extend to recreational study – much OCN work is with 'outreach' centres where leisure pursuits can be taken to a high standard, and the chance to have competence accredited may attract some clients.

OCN programmes are accredited at four levels, levels 2–4 being equivalent to NVQ levels 1–3, while OCN level 1 is below NVQ level 1. This can be particularly useful for some adults, allowing positive feedback and encouragement at an early stage. Where programmes are unit-based, clients may achieve the same or different units at two or more levels, so that different individual needs and abilities can be met effectively within the same programme.

In-fill

'In-filling' adult clients onto standard mainstream full-time or part-time courses is still used to offer access to vocational programmes, particularly where traditional (e.g. 16-plus) student numbers are falling. Sometimes this has delayed the demise of courses not otherwise viable. Such practice may not meet adult client needs, especially where clients join the programme when it has been underway for some time, and drop-out rates have tended to be high:

> It is important to note that the problem of drop-out from in-fill courses is not perceived in terms of inappropriate provision ... From the viewpoint of managers of the college, the unemployed are often viewed as inappropriate students. (Supporting the Unemployed in Further Education, FEU REPLAN, 1989.)

Except for very well-prepared clients, in-fill is unlikely to be effective unless linked with (a) diagnostic and induction programmes; (b) delivery methods that offer individual flexibility and choice within the learning programme; (c) personal tutor support with regular review of progress (see the section on incremental approach later in this chapter).

'21 hour rule'

Many 'access' courses are offered on the basis of limited attendance so that the unemployed can attend without losing benefit. Local operation of what used to be called the '21 hour rule' can vary and may affect access, since claimants are expected to show they are 'actively seeking work'. In colleges where access work is well developed, problems are usually avoided by close co-operation with local benefit offices[3]. Commitment to a long-term course may be seen as evidence that a client is not actively seeking work, and availability of short-term unit credit is thus especially important. In some important NIACE REPLAN projects[4] where colleges and local UBOs collaborated, reports stressed certain types of activity which could lead to credit in, for example, NCVQ core skill or foundation GNVQs units:

- college 'jobshops' or job clubs
- work on job-search skills and student portfolios to document job-hunting activity
- seeking and finding ways in which those leaving the course for a job could complete their qualifications.

Role of access provision

Access provision has a number of advantages. These include a focus on the needs of particular groups, peer group support for individual clients, and the opportunity for staff concerned to gain experience of the needs and problems of the unwaged. They can also be offered, at least on a limited scale, without major changes in overall college structures or programme delivery methods.

However, even with flexible and open learning methods, the range of vocational qualifications offered by separate 'access' courses will be limited. Clients' confidence and achievement, and resources available to them may also be affected if they are not

---

3   See Case Studies 1 and 4
4   1990/91

seen as part of the college 'mainstream'. As flexible delivery and individual learning programmes develop across vocational sectors, the need for such provision will tend to reduce and, where it exists, it may be more closely integrated with other work.

The issue of integration with mainstream provision may arise particularly for students with special educational needs. The degree to which this may be appropriate or feasible will depend on, for example, the nature of the client needs, the degree of flexibility and expertise offered by mainstream teams, and the types of client and student service available at college level. Current practice suggests three main types of approach, all of which may be provided within the same institution:

- wholly separate programmes
- moving from separate to integrated provision – e.g. separate initial 'core' programme, with subsequent vocational option studies taken increasingly within mainstream groups, but links with 'core' tutors maintained by regular meetings/reviews within 'core' groups
- joining mainstream programmes from the start, but with individual client support provided by:
  - mainstream tutors specifically briefed/trained for this
  - regular meetings/tutorials with specially trained learner support tutors.

MODULAR AND UNIT-BASED DELIVERY

Introduction and definitions

Many clients, particularly the unwaged, may need to take away formal credit after a relatively short period of study. The growth of unit-based vocational qualifications makes this possible, and 'modular' delivery systems are being adopted in a growing number of colleges, as exemplified in the case studies in Chapter 4. This section puts forward three strategies for opening access to credit which are linked later in the chapter with learner services needed to support them, and followed by a review of access and GNVQs. However, there are important general issues of definition, and of relationships between 'modularisation' and access, which must be considered before looking at specific delivery strategies.

29

'Module' and 'unit' are not precise terms, and are often used to mean the same and/or quite different things. Words like 'block', 'segment' and 'division' may also be used to denote parts of a programme or qualification. In this report we are concerned with four main, and distinct, types of 'module'. These are defined below.

NVQ and GNVQ units. NVQ Units of Competence and GNVQ Units of Achievement are the major example of 'assessment modules'. Assessment modules are defined by outcomes, not processes, and can be achieved and credited individually and in any order. They do not presuppose any specific type of learning programme, whether in 'modular' form or not. NVQs and GNVQs are often described as 'unit-based', 'unit competence-based' or 'outcome-based', and consist entirely of 'assessment modules'. This can remove many barriers to access.

NVQs and GNVQs are not designed to prescribe the nature and sequence of the learning programme, and it is important to grasp that both the award and individual units can be achieved in any manner, over any period, so long as the candidate provides evidence that satisfies the unit elements and performance criteria in the range of contexts laid down by the specification. Where the specifications are turned into a standard 'course', and the whole learner group proceeds at the same pace through a defined sequence of activities, this is likely to limit access.

Teachers may base learning programmes directly on NVQ/GNVQ unit specifications and proceed unit-by-unit and element-by-element. Alternatively they may choose to group units and/or may find certain kinds of activities and learning sequences more effective than others, either generally or in particular contexts. Ideally, the design and sequence of learning and assessment activities is geared to learner needs, and may vary with each individual.

Course units. Courses for some qualifications, for example modular degrees and some professional programmes, may be broken down into 'modules' that consist of defined learning activities which must be completed and assessed for achievement of each module and of the qualification overall. The qualification may or may not allow for separate unit credit, but modules cannot be awarded unless the learner completes the required coursework.

30

Such modules are best defined as 'learning and assessment modules', were long associated (for example) with BTEC awards, and are probably the type of module with which many teachers in FE have been most familiar. Because of past practice teachers may tend to treat NVQ or GNVQ units as learning and assessment modules, and to assume that all students will achieve them through the same defined course activities, rather than recognising that different people may produce the necessary evidence from quite different activities and experiences.

College-based 'modular' blocks. It is now quite common practice to divide college programmes into self-contained blocks of (say) six or 12 weeks. This may be done at course or departmental level or, in some cases, at college level. If such programme blocks deliver assessment for credit, they are 'learning and assessment' modules; if they do not, they are simply 'delivery' or 'learning modules'. Each block may deliver a number of course or assessment units in their entirety, or may provide elements/evidence towards a number of units without necessarily satisfying all assessment requirements for each of them.

The number of units in a block can vary considerably since NVQs may comprise anything from four to 16 or more units, and NVQ (as opposed to GNVQ) units are not necessarily of equal size or weight. A typical number is two or three units, but some programmes may block single units. Possible variations in the design of modular blocks are considered further under 'Strategy 2: Modular Blocks' and the section on flexible access and GNVQs, below.

Blocked programmes may be designed to cover more than one type of award (e.g. units from GNVQs, NVQs, academic or other vocational qualifications) and/or to offer students a choice between these. While this is a complex matter that involves mapping learning and assessment activities against the detailed specifications and requirements for each qualification, a number of colleges are developing programmes of this type.

Modular blocks may depend on a given sequence (e.g. first, second and third parts of a 'course year'). However, in this report 'Block' and 'Blocking' are used to mean learning programmes that do not depend on sequence – a learner may enter and take them in any order.

College-based learning and assessment modules. Some colleges are building their own system of 'modules'[5] which may, like NVQ units, be delivered within 'modular' blocks. Such modules may be based on NVQ or GNVQ units, other qualifications or non-certificated programmes. A modular block would usually cover a number of such modules.

Sometimes an open or flexible learning pack (e.g. for an NVQ/GNVQ unit) may be described as a 'module'. Where this includes provision for formal assessment it is a 'learning and assessment module'; otherwise it is simply a 'learning module'.

'Modularisation' and access

There is a current tendency to promote 'modular' delivery structures, often at institutional level. There may be good reasons for this which have nothing to do with opening access, though it is often wrongly assumed that the latter is an automatic result. Modular programmes do not necessarily improve access; for example:

- where modules are merely stages in a 'course' of defined length that may only be entered at a certain point
- if modules can only be achieved in a given sequence and the client cannot choose when or where to begin
- if separate unit credit is not awarded on completion of a module.

Flexible or 'resource-based' learning (RBL) is probably the most powerful strategy for open access. Some may question whether it should be termed a 'modular' approach since, at any given time, individual students may be working towards quite different units. Indeed, there are cases where existing RBL provision has become constrained by a college initiative on 'modularisation' – flexibility has been lost and entry become limited to each 'modular block' at three fixed points in the year.

Whether modular structures improve access depends on a range of supporting initiatives which need to be developed alongside

---

5   See for example Case Studies 2 and 3

changes in the structure of programme delivery. These supporting initiatives are considered in the section on learner services.

The following three sections describe and illustrate three types of approach which draw on current and developing practice: resource-based, modular blocks and incremental approach. All can offer multiple entry points during the year and deliver short-term unit credit. However, only the second involves a programme that is necessarily structured in 'modular' form. In practice the three overlap and are likely to do so more as flexible methods are further developed. At the same time they offer different starting points for colleges and programme teams.

Strategy 1: RESOURCE-BASED APPROACHES

Resource-based approaches cover a wide spectrum. They may be institution-wide or set up for part of one programme. Common elements are:

- increased learner control and choice of what is learned, by what method, with whom and when
- space, equipment and materials dedicated to a range of activities and information related to defined needs
- learning facilities accessible at most times of the day/week (preferably including lunch, 'twilight' and evening hours)
- staff who offer counselling, advice, feedback and assessment
- may be accessible for certain purposes on 'drop-in' basis, but more likely by appointment so that learners' needs are met (otherwise (s)he may have to wait, or return later)
- likely to be linked with client action plans, clearly specified and agreed outcomes or objectives, negotiated programmes.

Approaches vary both in flexibility and in the range and type of resources offered. Current practice in vocational sectors tends to include the following:

- client can enter and leave the programme at any stage, and choose which (e.g. NVQ) units to pursue and learning pace
- well-developed workshop resources and carefully planned and managed activity, linked with work-based tasks and competences
- individual induction, diagnosis, action planning and guidance

- guidance packs on the programme and on resource centre facilities, coupled with flexible learning materials and task descriptions for each unit
- resource-based facilities staffed as many days and hours as possible
- assessment of skills, competences or objectives available (within reason) on demand
- completed units and assessments are accredited as achieved
- depending on programme, client may pursue one unit at a time, two or more in parallel, or several together through integrative methods.

EXAMPLE 1: Hairdressing (NVQ level 2)

Assessment is by observation in college salon or at work. There are also written assessments set by college staff from City and Guilds question banks (monitored by City and Guilds). The whole programme can be salon-based for those not employed or on YT/adult training, and resource-based learning is common. Similar approaches are used in some case study colleges (see Chapter 4), but this example is from one of many other colleges using such methods:

- *the salon is open daily from 9.00am–4.30pm and it is planned to open evenings, with technician staff if tutors cannot be programmed*
- *open learning packs have been written to cover 'underpinning knowledge' for each of the 11 NVQ units, and can be used at home or college*
- *roll-on/roll-off is common and clients have action plans and personal programmes of work and assessment*
- *work experience can usually be arranged for clients not employed; team members train workplace assessors and help in workplace assessment (they would like more from employers, who often prefer to leave assessment to tutors)*
- *self-assessment (for each element of competence) and frequent tutor review are central to the programme; students are helped to take charge of their own learning and to decide when they are ready for a unit assessment*
- *units can, at least in theory, be taken in any order, although there are some obvious groupings; discussion with the trade has led to six 'take-away' sets of two to four units, each giving competence in a possible job area (e.g. shampooist)*
- *staff report that managing activities and meeting diverse needs means careful planning, imagination and quick responses*
- *an end of course exam (NOT part of the NVQ) has been laid on for younger full-time students in response to parents' wishes.*

35

EXAMPLE 2: Construction NVQs

There is a very wide range of Construction NVQs at levels 1–3, though currently only for operative and craft occupations, with CITB and City and Guilds acting as the sole joint Awarding Body. NVQs in Building Site Supervision and Management (levels 3 and 4) have also been accredited. Colleges are major providers of Construction NVQs, and those involved generally offer some or all of the main craft areas (e.g. Bricklaying, Carpentry and Joinery, Painting and Decorating, Plastering), and may also offer associated trades such as Plumbing, Gas Installation, Heating and Ventilating). Assessment for each unit has two main elements:

- an externally set, internally assessed, City and Guilds written test of 'underpinning knowledge'
- competence assessment through CITB Skills Tests at approved centres, which include many colleges; these tests are expensive and likely to be beyond the means of anyone not funded in some way.

Resource-based learning is well developed at a number of colleges and may involve, for example:

- workshop areas based on NVQ units or areas of competence, with members of staff on hand to provide assistance and supervision as required
- clients choose the units they want, and move from area to area as needed (taking CITB competence tests when ready)
- a flexible learning 'module' or pack for each unit, which includes:
  - explanation of principles, knowledge and practice, with references to further material available in a resources centre (see below)
  - example written test items
  - practical activities to carry out in the workshop
  - assignments and projects linking practical skills with their contexts to help develop understanding
  - self-assessment activities
- a resources centre with a variety of materials which students can access for assignment and project work
- 'learning modules' may include assessment packages which provide for assessment on site (e.g. through work on the college fabric or at the workplace) rather than at the college test centre.

EXAMPLE 3: NVQs in other vocational areas

Approaches similar to those outlined for Construction and Hairdressing can be developed for Business Administration NVQs. Some colleges have both 'model offices' where students can practise their skills, and 'real' functioning offices which provide business services for other parts of the college. The latter may also provide services to outside clients on a commercial basis or, in a few cases, may be an additional and separate business facility. While it is a complex task to balance business requirements against student needs and ensure appropriate supervision, such facilities can provide a basis for flexible, resource-based delivery. This is likely to call for:

- *unit-based learning packs which include (e.g.):*
  - *a range of activities that students can carry out in the model or practice office*
  - *learning assignments to develop knowledge and understanding*
  - *self-assessment activities to help students decide when they are ready to be assessed formally for unit elements*
- *marketing and selling services that provide opportunities for students to demonstrate practised skills required for NVQ units*
- *negotiating and timetabling assessment opportunities in the 'real' and/or commercial office, as far as possible in response to individual student needs.*

Hospitality and Catering can offer the same kind of opportunities in colleges whose facilities have been approved as a 'realistic work environment' for the purpose of delivering NVQs. However, perhaps even more than with Business Administration, how much flexibility can be offered to meet individual needs for particular units and assessment at any given time must be affected by the need to staff and manage complex commercial operations and ensure customer satisfaction.

EXAMPLE 4: Science GNVQs

Science GNVQs have been piloted and will be generally available from September 1994. They are likely to prove popular and their specifications stress scientific methods and activities that apply them. One pilot college has taken advantage of these specifications by:

- *equipping very large areas with facilities needed to carry out all the main kinds of activity required, and providing access for many students*
- *designing activities, assignments and related unit packages which enable students to learn independently, under appropriate supervision*
- *planning for flexible, individual learner-based delivery as far as possible, with the possibility of providing wholly resource-based provision for some students in the medium term.*

Strategy 2: MODULAR BLOCKS

Block delivery of programmes is used in most vocational sectors, including those for which NVQs or GNVQs are not yet available in colleges. 'Assessment modules' (e.g. NVQ and GNVQ units) offer the best opportunities for credit within blocks but 'course units/modules' (e.g. BTEC) are also delivered in this way. Main features of block delivery are:

- the whole award programme is divided into several 'blocked' periods (usually 6 or twelve weeks each) over the year (these may or may not coincide with terms)
- blocks are designed so that they can be offered and taken in any sequence
- within each block the programme may be 'integrated' or units may be offered in parallel
- each block is designed for maximum credit in terms of units that can be achieved during the block (it may not always be possible to deliver complete units)
- clients are generally accepted only at the beginning of each block, although clients seeking access between blocks may be offered:
  - counselling, diagnosis and action planning
  - induction activities and/or core skills workshops
  - open learning unit packs
- at the end of each block, achievement is reviewed and each student or client is accredited with units and/or competences achieved
- access and choice are increased if alternative blocks can be run in parallel.

Resource-based approaches may be used within blocks to allow the learner to plan his or her own programme, but learning is likely to be more structured. However, it may not always be easy for clients to confine their study to one or more units covered in the block. This problem is most pronounced where 'integrated' approaches are used – as in many BTEC programmes and quite often in GNVQ and/or NVQ programmes which replace them – but also arises where units are delivered separately in NVQs or GNVQs. Some reasons for this are outlined below with particular reference to NVQs. Similar problems can arise with GNVQs and are covered in the section on flexible access and GNVQs below.

Each NVQ unit should comprise a group of competences which relate to a specific job function. Although such functions should to a degree 'stand alone', groupings have been designed for assessment and not for training programmes. As a result they may not fall neatly into learning blocks and teachers can find that grouping them for delivery is not always an easy task. For example:

- some units may need to be included in each block (e.g. health and safety, or any that deal with foundation skills)
- in order to prepare students for NVQ assessment, other skills (e.g. learning skills, personal effectiveness) and understanding (e.g. industry, workplace and job context) may need to come into each block – it must be decided what is needed and how to include it
- job competence is best learned in the context of the whole job (through work experience or, for example, in a college hairdressing salon)[6] – to limit learning to specific functions or even parts of these may be seen as artificial
- some units may be based on specific skills which do not fall clearly into job functions but are spread across them
- student/client experience and needs (e.g. short-term access or full programme) may conflict and call for different unit groupings
- option streams within NVQs may mean coping with different numbers of units common to different numbers of NVQ streams.

Programme teams are developing ways of tackling these and other issues. Some are outlined below and others are illustrated in the examples which follow.

Induction programmes

These may include (a) material common to all blocks and (b) an introduction to the block in question. Ideally there will be one self-study pack for (a) and another for (b). Entrants between blocks

---

6 All hairdressing job functions and activities are likely to be going on at the same time in a college salon. For this reason unit blocking is unlikely to be used, except at the level of the individual student

will be able to use both and, if (a) includes diagnostic material and assignments, to agree further work with a tutor if needed – core skill workshops or, for those who are employed or have access to work placement, tasks to carry out during work experience.

Work placement

The need to set learning in the context of the whole job, especially for short-term clients, can be met by having work placement in each block. Those with work experience (employed, YT and adult trainees, unemployed/ unwaged with prior experience) can be set tasks that use it to draw out job contexts. Each block can also include group activity to link and review job functions and experience.

Flexible methods

Resource-based methods and flexible learning packs for units or parts of units can enable learners to pursue individual programmes. These may, where desired, focus on completing given units within the block. At the same time such methods can free tutors to give more time to individual client needs for learning and assessment.

EXAMPLES

Business Administration (NVQ levels 1–2): Introduction

New NVQs in Administration (previously Business Administration) were accredited by NCVQ to Awarding Bodies in March 1994. These have the same number of units as their predecessors at level 1, but at level 2 there is now only one NVQ which consists of eight common mandatory units and a further (optional) unit from a choice of seven. Examples below are based on outgoing NVQs in Business Administration, but apply in principle to the new NVQs. Certificates for outgoing NVQs can still be awarded for current students until April 1995 (level 1) and April 1996 (level 2).

Blocking has been common for Business Administration NVQs. At level 1 these comprise nine units while at level 2 there are three overlapping NVQs (Administrative, Financial and Secretarial). At level 3 there is a single title (Administration) which is less frequently offered than levels 1–2. Each level 2 NVQ has 15–16 units, of which seven or eight are taken from the nine at level 1, and four or more of the remaining units are common between the different titles.

Business Administration NVQs are offered by five different Awarding Bodies (BTEC, City and Guilds, LCCI, PEI, RSA) whose approaches in assessment and other areas (e.g. charges, documentation, etc.) vary, although unit specifications, assessment criteria and NVQs are identical. Colleges may offer more than one NVQ route (e.g. BTEC and RSA or LCCI).

Programmes generally deliver levels 1 and 2 together over one year (full-time, part-time or alternate blocks of work experience and college). Some question the separate role of level 1 in Business NVQs,[7] but a joint approach to levels 1 and 2 could be seen as a limit on access since it may prevent people who leave early from being credited with a level 1 NVQ.

---

7 In some sectors there are no plans to use level 1 or, in some cases level 2, because it is not felt to reflect a level of job competence. VET in Europe tends to recognise three basic levels which some equate with NVQ 2–4

Example 1: Blocks of six to seven weeks (BTEC)

In previous years students have been mainly full-time 16-plus and YT but the college now seeks to attract more adults. The programme team has divided the year into five blocks (A–E) to meet the needs of short-term clients, as well as full-time students and YT trainees.

- In each block there is a focus on specific units, but elements from a wider range of units are included.
- Most blocks contain both level 1 and level 2 units although, at present, Block A is mostly level 1 and Block E mostly level 2 (this may need revision for adult clients).
- Each block is designed round a major work-related (BTEC 'integrative') assignment that links the blocked units and relates them to broader contexts.
- Each block includes a week's work experience and some workplace assessment. Some students are placed in college offices or services.
- Each student has an action plan and profiled record of achievement. (S)he enters self assessments against each task and competence; achievement is regularly reviewed by tutors, with a major (summative) review at the end of each block.
- Much activity is resource-based and staff are able to attend to individual needs. Flexible learning materials are being developed.
- There is an induction pack for each block and a half day induction programme at the beginning of the block.
- For Block A there is a full induction guide to the programme and a week's induction. Similarly Block E has an extra week for review. The team are working on fuller induction packs for Blocks B–D.

Example 2: Blocks of 12 weeks (LCCI and BTEC)

The year is divided into three blocks, each extending over college holidays, with a final review week at the start of the next term. Intake is full-time students, YT and adult trainees. Because needs, experience, confidence and ability of students varies widely, three types of programme approach are offered:

- *'basic NVQ' route – using activities designed to meet minimum requirements of NVQ units*
- *LCCI route – using assignments provided by this Awarding Body which, the team feel, demand higher language skills than the NVQ competences alone*
- *BTEC route – this is linked with the GNVQ Business programme and uses BTEC 'integrative assignments'. Students may focus primarily on the GNVQ programme and pick up some NVQ units, or may concentrate on the NVQ. In either case it involves more work than the other routes and staff consider it more demanding.*

The team find that some adult returners feel the single office skill NVQ units are simplistic and prefer to develop competences in a broader context. The NVQ units are, on the other hand, seen to be ideal for motivating YT trainees who lack confidence.

A learning and assessment 'module' has been developed for each NVQ unit. These have been tried out with a number of employers as a basis for workplace assessment. Some have been developed as 'stand-alone' flexible learning packs. All include:

- *profile sheets to build informal records of progress (formative assessment) against each competence, with a formal statement of final achievement (summative assessment)*
- *a set of learning activities, materials and resources*
- *assessment activities, with some designed for work-based assessment.*

A number of 'support modules' have been produced with General Studies staff. They comprise materials and activities which may be supplemented by workshops, and at present cover basic and core skill areas such as job search, time management, numeracy, language, IT. They are used in a variety of ways:

- *to support development of basic and independent learning skills*
- *where tutors/students identify an individual need (e.g. in action-planning and review tutorials)*

- *by those wishing to obtain NCVQ core skill units: Communication, Application of Number, IT, Improving own learning and performance, Working with others. The first three are required for GNVQs, and NVQ clients may decide to seek unit credit for one or more of them.*

Much work is individual and resource-based, since students have different tasks and objectives. However, steps are taken to ensure that all experience both small- and large-group activity. While this is not specifically required for NVQ competences, the team see it as essential for overall competence, core skills and personal effectiveness.

Strategy 3: INCREMENTAL APPROACH

Some NVQ, GNVQ and other teams are adopting a gradual approach, using a staged plan to develop flexible delivery and promote access for adult clients. As the team builds flexible methods and materials it becomes easier to accept clients during the programme. Entry is negotiated with the individual client: it depends both on what the team can offer at a given stage in the plan and on the client's needs.

It may prove possible to cater for some clients but not others at a given stage. The plan is reviewed annually and priorities are set to meet needs identified over the previous year. Progress is quicker where the team can work with 'access' staff and/or link with an open workshop which offers diagnosis, core skill development and, especially, APL. Over a period the team may develop a fully resource-based 'roll-on/roll-off' system or may decide to bring in modular blocks.

Development plan checklist

The experience of colleges and teams working on flexible delivery and access suggests the following checklist for annual development plans. Much that is in the checklist is also relevant to teams using resource-based and block approaches.

STUDENT ASSIGNMENTS

- focus strongly on developing independent learning and core skills, and provide materials and individual learner support for them
- develop task-based and activity-based work to maximum degree, and map assignments clearly against unit elements and outcomes
- clarify evidence/outcomes to be produced by each assignment and make maximum use of learner's work and other experience
- ensure that the staff team shares specifications for all student assignments, and discusses their design
- review task and assignment design with students and clients
- refine assignments that are successful so that they can be done with minimum supervision

- develop student packs for tasks or assignments and relate these to units – include clear briefing and guidance, 'underpinning knowledge' and other relevant materials

ASSESSMENT

- design initial assignments and diagnostic materials to identify students' initial achievements and needs (e.g. for core skills)
- ensure that students (as well as staff) are familiar with unit specifications and criteria at as early a stage as possible
- use individual action-planning sessions to agree targets and learning activities geared to unit specifications
- produce guidance for student self-assessment and forms for recording this (peer assessment can also be included)
- build in regular student–tutor review of individual progress, with profiling system that ensures clear evidence of progress and achievement
- encourage learners to collect their own evidence against unit specifications, and claim units/elements when they feel they are ready.

RESOURCES

- develop activity areas, equipment and materials needed for task-based parts of the course
- extend information sources and materials (written, visual, video, computer-based, etc.) needed to support tasks and assignments
- review use of resource areas, materials, etc., and develop provision as necessary to ensure maximum individual access.

ACCESS AND INDUCTION

- prepare information on what is offered to access clients and liaise with access staff on format and distribution – review and up-date regularly
- identify likely client needs and design induction programme, for delivery by or with access staff where possible
- develop induction pack for individual client use, review regularly and modify in light of experience

- build diagnostic and (self-) assessment materials on important skill areas into induction programme and/or pack
- consider producing induction packs for individual units or groups of units.

The aim of the Development Plan is to lay a base for learning materials and packs that can be used by individual clients. Packs may include materials for group and interactive tasks to be set up by tutors and/or students at appropriate stages. A complete pack will be largely 'self-standing' and will include assessment materials. However:

- materials can be used at an earlier stage of development, and can be tried, tested and improved with the 'main group' or individual students
- packs can be produced one at a time and be offered to adult clients (as well as the 'main group'), together with tutorial support
- as complete packs are developed, more tutor time is available to support and advise access clients and other students.

REVIEW OF STRATEGIES

Resource-based strategies offer most opportunities for short-term unit credit, for flexible entry and for individual learning programmes. However, a number of colleges featured in case studies are using modular blocks as a way of moving towards more flexible delivery. Unless all blocks are offered in parallel (this has been done for some programmes) blocking limits unit choice, and access clients may have to follow a programme which is not structured to their needs. At the same time blocking enables a team to proceed towards more open delivery in a measured rather than once-for-all way:

- flexible methods can be developed within blocks and resource-based approaches may be introduced initially for a single block
- flexible learning packs and individual programmes can gradually be developed to allow clients to take units not necessarily covered by the current block(s).

Incremental approaches also offer staged development without the work of designing blocks. However, they may take time to attract access clients, impetus may be lost and the process may fail to take off. Blocked programmes, if well publicised, are likely to benefit from increased adult entry that tends to follow perceived improvement in access. Success for incremental approaches may depend on links with access programmes and workshops. These can offer both a source of potential clients and a stimulus to further development needed to meet their needs.

LEARNER SERVICES

Case study 3 in Chapter 4 shows how the concept of 'achievement-led institutional development' has been used to shift attention from courses to the services needed to support learner achievement. The degree and pace of change towards learner-centred services and flexible delivery will vary between colleges and will depend on local conditions. However, learner services are an essential partner to flexible programmes. Their joint effect under the NVQ/GNVQ framework is to support:

- access for wider groups and a wider ability-range of both adults and young people
- quicker progress for individuals, based on recognition of previous achievement and programmes tailored more to individual need.

Many colleges have established or are developing a range of systems and services to support access and learner achievement. These include admissions services, student counselling and guidance, core skill workshops, recording achievement, APL and open and flexible learning centres. The case studies in Chapter 4 as a whole show a variety of approaches to these services, and this section provides a brief survey of some of the main types.

Admissions

As 'access' client enrolments and programme entry points increase there is a need to extend admission services. Methods used may depend on factors such as whether independent educational guidance is offered locally and by whom, what types of 'access' programme the college provides, how many sectors and vocational qualifications are open to flexible access, relevant staff skills and expertise, etc. Approaches include:

- access programmes timed to precede cross-college starting points (each term or more often) for course 'blocks',

designed for clients wishing to pursue vocational qualifications for any sector or level
- induction programmes offered in the same way for specific vocational qualifications or for a whole vocational sector
- open learning workshops which offer diagnosis, guidance, basic skill development programmes, induction to certain courses, flexible learning packs and other services; experience of such workshops may lead to:
  - college-wide admission centres open daily through the year and staffed to offer and/or call on initial learner services as needed – an admission centre may have close links or share space with an open learning workshop.

Such approaches are not mutually exclusive – all may be offered within a college. The degree of choice open to clients, and the extent to which their needs are likely to be met will be affected by the range of services and expertise offered at college level: it is more difficult to develop these at course or sector level and it may be hard to avoid the temptation to 'capture' clients for a programme which may not be best suited to them.

Action planning

Levels of action planning. Individual action planning has a central role in access to vocational programmes and in enhancing learner achievement. It is important to distinguish these two levels of action planning:
- *initial action plans* concerned with diagnosis of an individual's needs, prior achievement, career and progression plans, and overall learning programme geared to these – such plans may be facilitated and agreed by careers and adult guidance officers, YT managing agents, and school or college staff at institutional or programme level
- *individual action planning within programmes* to set targets for the next stage of learning and assessment, agree methods, and review achievement since the last planning and review session. This process is central to the delivery of NVQs and GNVQs, and should relate back to initial action-planning.

Approaches to action planning. Some colleges have already introduced action planning as standard practice for all students and clients. While begun by generalist guidance staff, details of the programme to be followed are worked out with specialists in the vocational area. Action planning is closely linked with APL and other learner services outlined below, and its value to clients will increase as access to these improves. It is likely to involve:

- an initial counselling and diagnostic stage, which may take an existing action plan as its starting point. In some colleges this may be included in an induction programme for a particular course, assuming the client has already decided on a specific programme
- a review of needs in the light of what the college (or other providers) can offer
- a learning contract which covers the programme, learning and assessment methods to be used and any further matters, such as work experience or workplace assessment, choice of options, etc.
- regular action-planning and review at programme level, carried out by vocational programme staff, or by personal or other tutors with the role of supporting vocational teams and students in this way
- additional learner support (e.g. core skill workshops) to which learners can be referred where action planning and review sessions show specific needs
- modification or updating of initial action plan made where required (e.g. change of programme or options) by agreement with appropriate tutors
- exit counselling where the initial action plan and achievement before leaving are reviewed, the learning programme evaluated, and future action discussed and agreed.

Databases for action planning. Wirral Metropolitan College (see Chapter 4) has decided to enter on a computer database details of all programmes and units, delivery modes and assessment methods, together with student action plans. This is being backed by an 'Expert System' to support admissions staff and increase student involvement in choosing learning programmes. The client inputs data on age, experience, qualifications, preferred learning mode, vocational interests, etc., to obtain guidance on training programmes which could meet his/her needs.

The NVQ database (available by annual subscription from NCVQ) now contains full details of a very large number of vocational qualifications, including all NVQs and GNVQs with their

51

unit specifications. While many colleges have acquired the database it is often not accessible to those who need to use it. It can be used by clients and tutors to match unit competences and outcomes against clients' past experience and future needs, decide on personal programmes and agree methods to achieve them. Current versions of the database include facilities for local notes to be made against NVQs, and for individual action plans and records against each unit and element.

APL and related services

Definitions. Approaches to assessing clients on entry have developed in response to (a) the needs of 'access' clients and (b) the NVQ framework, which separates assessment from learning programmes. Terms such as APL, APA, APEL have become attached to some but not all of these approaches and, although APL may now be the most common, there are still shades of meaning in its use. Some processes and activities associated with 'APL' are described below.

(1) The formal process of awarding unit accreditation, certified by an awarding body for prior learning, experience or achievement, on the basis of evidence provided by the candidate and/or assessments carried out by staff qualified to do this (e.g. at an 'APL Centre').

(2) Recording achievement of elements within a unit (without the formal certification that is only given for a unit), so that the client need only be assessed for the remainder to achieve unit credit. This may include agreeing further evidence and/or learning experiences required to achieve unit credit or credit for a whole award.

(3) Recording evidence towards elements within a unit, and identifying further evidence required – also likely to be coupled with an agreed learning and assessment plan to achieve unit credit.

(4) Reviewing and assessing prior experience, skills and/or achievement on entry to a learning programme in order to decide, e.g.:
   - any specific types of support the learner may need during the programme (e.g. core skills)

- content and length of learning programme (e.g. areas or parts of the programme that need or need not be included).

(5) Assessing or diagnosing core or basic skills to determine client needs, level of entry, suitable sector or vocational qualification (e.g. where clients are on a 'return to work/study' programme which includes diagnosis, core skills, vocational qualification and/or work experience 'tasters').

Using APL. Any of the above processes may occur in the course of action planning, and they may well overlap. Some would restrict the term APL (accreditation of prior learning) to the award of full unit credit and would describe (2)–(5) as 'initial diagnostic assessment' (IDA). However, APL is commonly applied to 'top-up' of partial credit by a shortened learning programme and further assessment, and it is rare for clients to achieve full awards through APL without significant further evidence and learning activity.

APL and diagnostic assessment imply a system whose focus is the needs, objectives and achievement of individuals. Learning programmes, delivery and assessment methods are tailored to ensure maximum achievement rather than to maximise the time students spend in college. Some colleges have established dedicated APL centres for particular qualifications, but these are extremely resource intensive, and assessment by APL is more likely to save clients' time than money. More often 'IDA' is developed as a general aid to access and to individually tailored programmes that can be provided through modular, resource based and other flexible approaches to delivery.

The NCVQ pack *Credit for Competence* (1990) explains APL method and gives examples of its use. In his commentary Gilbert Jessup argues that, while standards must be maintained, there is a tendency to demand more evidence than is necessary to demonstrate competence. Such a tendency is self-defeating since it makes APL less attractive to clients and more costly than it need be. Other methods used by colleges to reduce the intensive staff resource needed for APL and/or IDA include:

- standard diagnostic tests (many can now be obtained from other colleges and/or commercially) and 'expert systems'

- group reviews and workshops on prior achievement and experience, including domestic, leisure and voluntary activity, as well as work and educational learning and experience
- take-away APL packs which help clients review their past experience and identify knowledge, skills and competences they have acquired, and include self-assessment activities.

Importance of records of achievement. APL and/or IDA may be used:

- on entry – either to shorten a programme or to give credit independent of any programme of study
- on exit – to carry credit forward for future APL when a client leaves a programme without other formal credit.

To be effective the latter calls for regular reviews of progress and well-evidenced records of progress and achievement, clearly related to skills and competences. This process is crucial to effective individual programmes, is generally required by Awarding Bodies for NVQs and GNVQS, and is a major issue for most teams delivering these qualifications.

Open and flexible learning

'Open' and 'flexible' learning are terms used to describe a wide range of overlapping methods and approaches, from resource centres to distance learning. While all such methods can be used to enhance access to unit credit, two specific types of service have been referred to in this handbook and are reviewed below:

- open or flexible learning centres and workshops
- open or flexible learning packs for individual use.

Open learning workshops. Learning workshops have been used for some time to provide support and development in core skill areas such as communication and number. In many colleges these now include other skills such as study skills, languages and, especially, IT, and may also offer 'flexible study' for particular courses and qualifications. This has led to 'drop-in' provision which may offer, for example: diagnostic tests; tutor guidance, counselling and assessment of work; basic skill development programmes; learning materials for GCSE and other qualifications, for workshop or home use; video, audio and computer-based learning resources.

In some colleges these centres have been developed to include a full range of learner services:[8] centre staff work with a growing number of vocational teams whom they may assist with admissions counselling and induction, action planning and APL, 'flexible' learning and assessment packages, and support for GNVQ candidates on core skill units. Open learning centres can be an effective base for developing expertise in 'access' counselling and other learner services – part-time staffing by members of mainstream sector teams can help spread experience across the college and lay the foundation for college-wide services. Their role in supporting core skills in GNVQ programmes can also be crucial, since vocational teams may not include the necessary expertise in all core skill areas; as well as providing workshop and tutorial support, open learning staff may advise or help on the design of assignments which will enable students to develop and apply core skills in vocational contexts.

Flexible learning packs. Learning packages for individual modules or units may have a range of roles and objectives. In many cases they may simply cover 'underpinning knowledge' and prepare students for written or oral assessment of this. However, they may also contribute more directly to the achievement of competence (or to GNVQ elements of achievement). How far they do this will depend on the nature of the units concerned, assessment requirements and pack content and method. Teams in various sectors have produced 'stand alone' packs for suitable units which include, for example:

- video and other resources to help in the analysis of processes, and to provide demonstrations (or even practice) of practical skills
- interactive materials or computer software to develop and test understanding and intellectual skills
- briefings for practical tasks and projects, and criteria for reviewing and assessing competences in these
- materials for group simulation and role play
- briefing to prepare students for work experience, together with tasks to be carried out during work placement

---

8   See case studies 2 and 4, Chapter 4

- guidance and frameworks for self-assessment – e.g. for competences at the workplace or in the workshop.

FLEXIBLE ACCESS AND GNVQs

GNVQ structure and assessment requirements

GNVQs at Foundation (level 1) and Intermediate (level 2) consist of six vocational units, while Advanced GNVQs (level 3) have 12 vocational units. All GNVQs also include three core skill units whose delivery should be 'integrated' in work for vocational units – i.e. vocational assignments should include opportunities for development and assessment of the core skills. Although GNVQs may be delivered and achieved over any period, Advanced GNVQs are expected to take two years of full-time study and the other levels one year. Thus six vocational units will normally be covered over a year's programme.

The primary assessment requirement is a portfolio of evidence that satisfies the elements, performance criteria and range specified in each unit. However, for most mandatory vocational units students must also pass a short, externally-set written test. This means that a GNVQ candidate normally has to take three such tests over a year's programme. Since tests can be retaken as many times as necessary and are currently available four times a year, many GNVQ programmes are designed so that candidates complete work on at least some units by the first round of tests in January.

The three bodies that award GNVQs (BTEC, City and Guilds, RSA) all place strong emphasis on initial individual assessment, action planning, individual learning programmes, access to assessment and equal opportunities. This makes for good opportunities to open access for adults who may be interested in these awards, and/or in obtaining unit credit towards them. However, the latter depends on the unit delivery structure adopted by the particular GNVQ staff team.

Issues of unit-based delivery

While there are some general differences between vocational areas, almost every conceivable unit delivery structure is in current use, for example:

- six units delivered separately over the whole year, in parallel
- three blocks of two units, or two blocks of three

- four mandatory units in the first semester, the second given to two optional units and any further evidence needed for mandatory unit and core skill unit portfolios
- mix of 'short fat' and 'long thin' unit programmes
- unit-based sequential, i.e. 'modular blocks' consisting of a single unit
- a series of 'integrated' projects/assignments that include elements of several units (typical in Art and Design, but also used in other areas)
- resource-based approaches, though not as yet generally developed to allow clients choice of which units to work on at a given time.

Although many GNVQ programme teams outside Art and Design currently deliver all units separately, relationships between learning needs and unit content can make it hard to deliver complete units in a given sequence, for example:

- successful completion of some units may call for understanding and skills acquired in connection with several other units
- some units may be best worked on throughout the programme because they interact with other units delivered at particular stages
- realistic vocational activities and assignments are likely to relate to elements in several units
- assignments designed for a specific unit may often provide evidence for other units
- one college started with a policy of sequential single unit blocks to maximise adult access, but moved to two-unit modular blocks because of problems experienced with a single unit approach.

Delivery structures are linked with the kinds of learning and assessment activities or assignments used in GNVQ programmes. These are of three main types: unit-based (relating to one unit only), integrated (relating to elements from several units) and unit-focused (designed for a particular unit but also providing some evidence towards elements in other units). There is some evidence that an effective GNVQ programme is likely to include all three types, though the balance between these will vary between vocational area, and with staff preferences and learner needs.

Opening access to GNVQs

Currently many colleges and GNVQ teams are concerned to offer unit credit for those who leave programmes early. This is leading to growing adoption of two main models that provide for this:

- modular blocks of two or three units, which may be delivered separately or through integrated assignments
- programmes which adopt an integrative model but provide for 'staggered completion' of units – each assignment covers two or more units, but the primary focus switches at various stages in the programme.

Although these models deliver unit credit during the programme year, they do not necessarily allow clients access after the programme has 'started'. However, some colleges are implementing policies on this, are providing learner services to support such clients, and GNVQ teams are working towards self-contained blocks backed up by appropriate learning materials. In some cases they are also developing opportunities for clients to 'mix-and-match' GNVQ and NVQ units.

GNVQs are still at an early stage of implementation, and the main emphasis so far has been on full-time courses for young people at school or leaving school. There are also doubts in some quarters as to how far GNVQs may appeal to adults. However, there is sufficient evidence from those delivering GNVQs to adults that they can meet a variety of needs, for example:

- those wishing to change career, or start a new career, who are looking for a broad introduction to the area of work
- those interested in working towards a professional qualification or a degree, who prefer not take the academic A-level route
- returners looking for core skills and vocational 'tasters' at a more basic level (e.g. GNVQ Foundation).

It is likely to be some time before there is a body of experience on the most effective ways to structure programmes and deliver units to meet the needs of a variety of students and clients. Young people may need the realism of context that integrated delivery can offer. Adults with greater experience may find it easier to set the limited objectives of a particular unit in a broader context, and so meet the unit criteria at an earlier stage in the programme. The unit-based structure of GNVQs, their emphasis on learner-centred approaches, growing experience of modular and flexible delivery, and the need to attract adult clients should combine to provide more flexible access – whether through modular blocks or resource based delivery, or through a mixture of the two – in the medium term.

CHAPTER 4

College Case Studies

INTRODUCTION

The case studies were chosen to illustrate a range of responses to the need for increased adult access. Three of them are from colleges included in the first edition (Peterlee, Cumbria College of Art and Design (CCAD) and Wirral), while two are new (Croydon and St Helens). They represent institutions of varied size (from some 30 to over 500 full-time teaching staff), different kinds of area (county, city and metropolitan), and contrasting communities (economically deprived to highly prosperous). Although they are not geographically representative and do not include all college types, it is suggested that they offer experience and approaches of direct relevance to most colleges.

Individual case studies cover varied levels of college activity and provide contrasting types of information in order to give a fuller picture of responses to change. Because of this they are not presented in standard form and do not invite direct comparisons. While all show institutional approaches to open access and flexible delivery, they illustrate three main kinds of focus and ways in which these interact. More than one of the following strategies may be pursued at the same time, or emphasis may shift between them at different points in development:

- institutional focus – overall change at institutional level designed to improve provision for all clients, and necessarily benefiting adults: Wirral, Croydon, St Helens
- mainstream programme focus – evolving structures geared to full-time or mainstream provision so as to increase accessibility for adults: CCAD especially, but also a focus in other colleges at different stages (e.g. Peterlee, St Helens)
- adult access focus – radical initiatives aimed at greater adult participation leading, in turn, to general changes that benefit all students: Peterlee especially, but also a crucial element at St Helens and elsewhere.

Contrasts between case studies result to a large degree from the type of institution and/or the researcher's focus in each case. However, the following features are of special note:

- the scale and success of Peterlee's activity in removing barriers to access and in attracting adults to the college
- the thoroughgoing and ambitious character of Wirral's plans to change the whole culture of the college, and the systematic way in which this is being carried through
- links at Croydon between market research, access and entitlement policies, providing a wide range of customer services, and the use of quality assurance systems to check that policies are implemented
- the variety of different practical initiatives at St Helens college and the way these have been brought together to improve both access and overall quality of provision
- CCAD's systematic recasting of staff roles and modular curriculum framework.

Although the colleges are at different stages of development towards client-centred provision and have different objectives and priorities, there are common themes that run through the case studies and are reflected in other colleges responding to the challenges which this publication has outlined. Some of these themes are highlighted below.

College Structure

- movement towards flatter management structures with more responsibility taken by middle management, in the context of clearly established institutional policies
- wider range of cross-college roles and posts, especially student services, industry liaison and curriculum development
- cross-college roles may be specific posts or a defined element in the role of individuals or groups of staff. Balance between these is likely to vary (contrast Peterlee and CCAD on the one hand with Wirral, St Helens and Croydon on the other).

Work with Adults

- strong provision for and experience of adult clients from (e.g.) ET/TFW to access courses, open learning workshops and other provision (CCAD is the one exception, though average age on many of its programmes is now over 21 and this is a high priority)

- specific senior management responsibility for developing work with adults and promoting adult access and markets.

Multi-Point Entry

- client entry to programmes at least three times a year (e.g. by modular 'blocking', roll-on-off or, as in the case of CCAD, induction available each term coupled with flexibility in programme delivery)
- movement towards continuous entry through open workshops, resource-based learning and college-wide admissions services.

Learner Services

- strong focus on guidance, diagnosis and APL – whether provided by open workshop, college admissions service, guidance tutors or programme teams
- production of 'stand alone' learning packs for units, including videos and computer software, and incorporating self-assessment exercises
- movement to college-wide, learner-centred assessment systems and services – including action-planning, continuous progress review and records of achievement.

Industry Links

- development of consultancy services and customised training for industry
- consulting with firms on detailed needs and job content, and working with them on design of programmes, learning and assessment activities
- aim to provide work experience and workplace assessment for all students who need it, including unwaged adults.

Case Study 1: PETERLEE TERTIARY COLLEGE

BACKGROUND: THE 'BREAD' PROJECT

Peterlee is the only further education college in East Durham, where there are also five 11–16 high schools and one 11–18 Roman Catholic comprehensive school. A tertiary college from 1984 its main focus for the next three years was developing full-time programmes for school leavers. However, in 1987 the college helped research 'The Smiths', a short BBC series about a Peterlee family's experience of unemployment, broadcast nationally in March 1987. This led to much local interest and to a greater awareness both of what was needed and of what might be done.

The result was the 'BREAD' project: Better Response in Education to Adult Demand, funded for 12 months by NIACE REPLAN, who also co-ordinated the East Durham Adult Learning Network. This linked the college with local government departments, local firms, voluntary interests including CAB and NACRO, and with the local UBO, Job Centres and DSS. The first step was to improve marketing and information, and to take provision to the client through, for example:

- town centre and mobile 'Opportunities Shops' giving advice and information on unemployment, finding out about adult learning needs, and staffed by Network members, college staff and unemployed adult students
- closer links with government agencies. The college set up stands in both Job Centre and UBO, held joint recruiting drives with them and, as a result, had an average of 10 new adult enrolments on part-time courses each day during the project
- four college 'outreach' centres set up and supported by the Network in response to mobile shop demands.

The second step was a new kind of provision to meet adult needs, which became known as the 'Honeycomb'. The college product design group met for two full days away from college, with a three-week gap between. It was agreed that the new product must:

- come in 'bite-sized' chunks – six-week units of two to three hours per week
- allow both progression and combination with other 'units', and lead to some form of certification
- include guidance and counselling on entry and progression, and be backed by a workshop that offered help with job-seeking and study skills, careers advice and personal guidance:

64

- to support students through their units
- to induct those wishing to join between unit start dates.

The result was a wide range of vocational units, many of them new. Each attracted a college certificate of achievement and, after a required number, access to external awards. Units were fitted into the 20 cells (four time-slots a day, five days a week) of the Honeycomb, and were repeated on different days and/or in different time-slots to maximise access. During the project college enrolments increased by 60 per cent, unwaged students by 90 per cent and adults on full time courses by 40 per cent.

The Honeycomb proved too costly to sustain once outside funding was withdrawn. However, the BREAD project was crucial in the college's development as an institution serving the whole community: it changed the client profile, and it involved most staff in a major curriculum development through which they acquired new skills in teaching adults and more flexible attitudes to programme delivery. It also underlined the need to:

- develop services that would maximise adult access and achievement at the same time as giving improved support to school leavers
- achieve greater flexibility of programme delivery within tight cost constraints.

SUSTAINING GROWTH IN ADULT PROVISION

Over the past three years the number of adult students at Peterlee College has increased by 300 per cent. The increase includes: adults on full- and part-time programmes; 'mainstream' provision and programmes designed specially for adults; many women returners with young children but also workers made redundant because of pit closures; people wishing to move from low- to better-paid jobs, and company employees for whom the college provides tailored programmes on site. It is linked with the development of new support services, a growing range of programmes and greater flexibility – each of which serves to attract more adult clients, who in turn provide a base for further curriculum and other development.

Support services

The following services have been developed over the past few years:

- a 'Student Services' centre open 9.00am–9.00pm Monday to Thursday and 9.00am–4.30pm on Fridays, supported by a 24-hour telephone hotline – it gives advice and guidance on courses, careers and employment, HE and FE opportunities, grants and benefits, study problems, relationships, health, money and housing, and offers diagnostic assessment and APL services

- a well-appointed and much-used 'Learner Services Centre' with library, computer stations, multi-media studio, excellent desk-top publishing provision, copying and cut-and-paste facilities and extensive study space
- numeracy and literacy workshops (the college has run two ALBSU projects – one based at the Learner Services Centre and the other for employees in local companies)
- an intensively-used college creche with space and staffing for over 50 children aged two to five, which is open from 8.45am–4.00pm and has led to a very significant increase in the number of full-time women students with young children
- ramps, chairlifts, lifts and other facilities to provide access for those with physical disabilities on both main college sites
- continued co-operation with and support from the local UBO over the attendance of unemployed adults on college programmes
- a College Company that provides a commercial consultancy for computer hardware and software, general support and training for those starting or developing small businesses (in conjunction with East Durham TEC), and offers training programmes for employed people both at the college and for companies on-site
- varied and developing provision for local community needs at three outreach centres in East Durham.

Programmes for adults

While adults form a significant proportion of students on many programmes at Peterlee, some have been developed for adults only. These include:

- full-time HE Access courses (10.00am–3.00pm) offering entry to vocational and academic degree programmes and validated by the University of Northumbria (student numbers have increased from 40 to 120 in recent years, and discretionary grants are currently awarded to those under 39)
- 'year 0' and/or first year of University of Sunderland degree courses in Health Studies, Engineering, Science and other subjects, which can be taken full-time or part-time, and for which adults can obtain mandatory grants
- an increasing range of TFW (previously ET) provision, offered by the college as Managing Agent
- full-time FE/vocational access courses lasting 12 weeks to six months providing core/study skills and vocational 'tasters'

- a range of job preparation and basic training programmes and workshops for those seeking employment, offered part- and/or full-time and lasting between a week and 12 months, with some providing certification or access to certificated courses
- some NVQ and other vocational programme groups run specifically for non-employed adults, e.g. Business Administration and Construction
- part-time programmes for employed adults in management, computerised business applications and other vocational areas and including A-level in Japanese.

Adult access to other programmes

A variety of college initiatives are helping to promote adult access, such as founding a local OCN branch, a local community action training and support group, close co-operation with the Countryside Commission, and a strong focus on funding from voluntary sources including the European Community. Adult access to mainstream programmes has been opened up by establishing normal 'class contact' for full-time programmes at 15 hours a week, and by developing some 'roll-on, roll-off' provision. The latter is based on resource-based workshop delivery rather than 'blocked unit' provision, is offered for NVQs in Administration, Catering, Construction and Hairdressing, and allows flexibility in both starting point and attendance mode. In some cases students may be accepted at any time, but entry points are more often at three- or six-week intervals, and Student Services staff may provide diagnostic or other activities to help prepare those waiting to start.

Adults joining full-time groups are not treated as 'in-fill' members, since staff have become very conscious of the needs of adult clients: curriculum delivery methods are increasingly flexible and a range of student and learner services offer support at individual level. Adults make full use of the latter both on their own initiative and in response to tutor referrals.

FLEXIBLE MAINSTREAM PATHWAYS

Work with adults has had a decisive impact on the overall structure of college provision. A timetable 'Matrix' embraces a high proportion of college programmes including NVQs, GNVQs, Diploma in Vocational Education, Access programmes, and some A-levels and GCSEs. It is based on a week that consists of five blocks of six hours, each programme taking a specified number of blocks, each of which comprises a mix of contact time and programmed activity. This allows students to mix-and-match the whole or parts of different programmes and qualifications on the basis of need and interest. One block (Block E) is kept free of formal programmes to allow flexible access to tutorials, core skill support, and a range of 'extension' studies and activities.

A crucial advantage of the Matrix is that students can access as few as one or as many as five 'blocks', so that there is no longer a real distinction between 'full-time' and 'part-time' modes. Some other ways in which programme flexibility and individual support have been developed are outlined below:

flexi-study is available for a number of qualifications (e.g. GCSEs). It is based on customised materials and tutorials timed to meet individual requirements

programme length: while there is some roll-on-off provision, 'standard' programmes are increasingly delivered in ways that allow individuals to proceed at their own pace. For example, some GNVQ and NVQ students achieve level 2 within two rather than three terms and move straight to level 3, so that (e.g.) both Intermediate and Advanced GNVQs may be achieved within two rather than three years

action planning and review is conducted on a 10-week cycle, when tutors review progress towards overall targets with each student and targets are agreed, including any change of programme and/or need for specific support over the next part of the cycle. This is in addition to short-term action planning and review which may occur in 'Block E', or needs that may be identified through student support and learner services

flexible delivery methods continue to be developed within individual programmes within the Matrix. For example, a resource-based approach is used for Art and Design Intermediate GNVQ with support and materials for the six units of the award available through the year, and several members of staff in the studio at any one time. Students can thus choose their own unit focus at any given time and can work at their own pace.

REMOVING BARRIERS TO ACCESS

From its experience of the 'BREAD' project, the college produced a simple 'Barriers Checklist' as an aid to work with adults. This has proved an invaluable reminder and reference point for the college's administrative, teaching and support staff, and for many others elsewhere. The checklist is reproduced here.

Bread Project Barriers Checklist

PERSONAL

	low confidence and self-esteem
	previous negative educational experience
	lack of information about what is available
	difficulty with reading and writing
	domestic responsibilities, such as children, disability or elderly relatives
	cultural and language difficulties
	social stigma attached to certain addresses, such as hostels, hospitals
	dependency on benefits and their related regulations
	low income, therefore low level of aspiration and mobility

GEOGRAPHICAL

	a community with no local college
	an area with infrequent and expensive transport, or no transport at all
	a 'no go' area in terms of personal safety, particularly at night
	a local education authority with no remission of course or examination fees
	or one with a limited or non-existent budget for discretionary grants for mature students

INSTITUTIONAL

	intimidating 'institutional' buildings
	hostile, unwelcoming reception areas
	authoritarian or unhelpful officials, lecturers, receptionists or other staff
	inappropriate or inadequate facilities for adults in terms of both learning and recreational spaces
	complex prospectuses and enrolment procedures
	no creche or childcare facilities
	no physical facilities for disabled or elderly students
	provision dominated by the demands of certain social or age groups
	provision dictated by professionals' views of needs
	stigmatised groups often find their position reinforced by separate or 'annexed' provision
	courses offered at times that suit staff only
	courses offered on site only
	information is in printed form, there is no built-in guidance, counselling and referral service
	entry requirements reflect formal traditional qualifications, do not take life experience into account
	courses are too lengthy
	courses have inflexible start and finish dates

Case Study 2: WIRRAL METROPOLITAN COLLEGE

COLLEGE AND CLIENTS

Wirral is a community college with about 2,000 full-time students on three main sites and some 60 'outreach' centres that account for a quarter of its 37,500 annual enrolments. Its work with the local community (including local business and 'access' clients) is varied, for example:

- Managing Agent for YT/ET, it covers sectors such as business, motor vehicles, hairdressing, but also sets up special programmes for individuals (e.g. violin making)
- a college bus takes computer training to 1,000 people a year, in their communities
- the Portfolio Service visits approximately 50 companies each year and can train company staff to be work-based trainers, assessors and verifiers
- the Business Support Unit arranges customised training for small businesses in computer applications, language training and accounts
- there is a range of access programmes including 'into work' courses for women, e.g. woodwork, plumbing, engineering, with play groups or paid childcare
- provision for the disabled is being improved and more attend each year – some from other areas whose colleges cannot provide for them
- the college catalogue provides details on fee remission
- the college has possibly the finest educational computer network in Europe with a comprehensive array of software packages, programming languages and CD-roms
- a wide range of student support services exist, e.g. finance, accommodation, counsellors, careers, admissions and student union.

Open Learning Workshops exist in mathematics and communications, together with a newly established Development Centre. The Development Centre can assist students in identifying their learning needs in the important core areas of communications, numeracy and information technology. Accreditation of prior learning (APL) in certain vocational areas is also available through the Centre.

STUDENT-CENTRED LEARNING

The college aims to become a new kind of institution: centring on learning rather than teaching, resourcing student achievement rather than courses. Management is convinced that this can be at least as economical as the

71

traditional FE college and has now organised its strategic planning around these principles, for example:

- radical restructuring, with a variety of new staff roles that do not include 'teacher' or 'lecturer'
- new and expanded learner services and resources, to form the basis of what the college offers
- assessment that is independent of learning, with learner choice of route (e.g. APL, open learning, self-directed learning)
- a modular system that spans the college and links common programme elements, including academic and vocational (see Learning Framework)
- resourcing a new Learning Centre to focus on new services for individual students (see Learning Centre).

Process of Change

A college bulletin notes:

> By and large it is still the case that syllabuses and lecturers constitute the conceptual centre and starting point for colleges; and that students are secondary. The student is still normally required to adjust him or herself to an established curriculum and mode of delivery ... the concept of a student-centred college replaces the idea that a college may be less mature than its students, which may as a result limit their achievements.

The college mission demands that high quality courses continue through the period of change, and that best current practice is retained in the new system. Change on all fronts is planned to support existing courses while, at the same time, laying the basis for new student services and modes of delivery.

NEW COLLEGE STRUCTURE

From first moves in 1987 the basis of the structure was complete by late 1989. Senior management was reduced and middle management's role enlarged: 11 departments were replaced by five faculties, and cross-faculty posts (e.g. core studies, curriculum development) strengthened. Some 70 Section Heads (SLs and PLs) have become the new middle managers, with charge of section budgeting and resourcing.

These changes released substantial funds which made possible the creation of a sixth faculty, College Services. This faculty is a major force for continuing change and development.

> ## College Services: Sections
>
> **Learner Services**
> **Marketing and Public Relations Unit**
> **Learning Resources**
> **Staff Services**
> **Training and Development**
> **Research and Development**
> **The Portfolio Service**

> ## Lateral Cross-College Posts
>
> **Manager – Staff Training**
> **Co-ordinator – European Social Fund**
> **Co-ordinator – Information Technology**
> **Manager – Mettnet Business Training**
> **Manager – Open Learning**
> **Manager – Extension Studies**
> **Manager – Assessment and Accreditation**
> **Co-ordinator – Information Technology**
> **Manager – Staff Development**

Learner Services

Learner Services has a key change agent role and a curriculum head. It is guided by a model 'learner pathway' which informs college development tasks. Examples include:

- college-wide admissions services to include clearly channelled information and advice
- initial assessment of students' learning needs
- vocational core to be defined and common core to be programmed across related courses
- establish records of achievement.

COLLEGE RESOURCES

The Learning Centre

The purpose-built Learning Centre is situated on the first floor of the Borough Road site and comprises:

73

- access to information on college-wide learning opportunities. College advisers are available to answer queries regarding the college's academic and vocational provision
- fully equipped and staffed communications and mathematics workshops. Students can improve basic skills or take a GCSE or City and Guilds by flexible study
- a careers service offering advice and guidance relating to courses in higher education, employment and further training opportunities
- a facility for students who wish to claim credit for their prior learning (APL) against a recognised qualification. An initial assessment service is also available to determine existing levels of ability in the important 'core' areas of communications, numeracy and information technology
- the dispensary has available for hire or purchase a wide range of open learning materials
- access to the finest education computing facility in Europe. Comprehensive business and programming software packages can be used for the production of assignments, analytical tools or as self-teaching aids. Over thirty CD-roms provide a vast array of research data
- quiet areas offering access to videos and audiotapes for individual use.

THE LEARNING FRAMEWORK

The Learning Framework is the college's system for harmonising the FE curriculum through outcomes and credit value. It provides a method for recording the gains that students make from their learning, i.e. a system for accrediting the full range of gains made by the learner as well as a system for credit accumulation and transfer within the institution. Developing the Learning Framework has been a continual process of refinement and modification as a consequence of the practical experience gained from implementing the system across the whole college.

The Learning Framework is aptly named – it was devised to facilitate learning and maximise achievement and, right from its inception, it has always had the students and their needs very firmly at the centre of its development. Although there are clear management and resourcing implications to be derived from such curriculum developments, the work on the Learning Framework has never lost sight of the fact that it is a dynamic educational tool designed to benefit the student.

Individual course tutors have themselves decided not only how their courses should be broken down into more manageable and coherent chunks of learning but also have defined the learning outcomes in such a manner as

74

to reflect the full range of gains. In addition, core skills units are also being developed at a number of different levels parallel to the subject-specific units and these are identified as associated core units on each unit specification. Furthermore a number of units are being developed which attempt to enhance the definition of the 'value added' dimension. These are 'effective worker' units, which describe the additional practice and experience which distinguishes a competent from a capable worker; and 'effective learner' units, which encompass those evaluative/analytical skills, and aspects of personal skills such as motivation, perseverance and time management, which differentiate more readily a learner who is likely to progress. Parallel with this work is the development of a set of units which describe certain specific aspects of the learning process and which are compatible with the elements described in Option E of the Further Education Funding Council's paper, *Funding Learning.*

Most of the curriculum has now been mapped onto the Learning Framework database and in addition, core skills units have been identified corresponding to the different programme levels, and a range of units have been developed which describe the processes involved in learning. All full-time programmes will have been operating on a credit basis from September 1993.

In addition, an achievement-based resourcing pilot, using the Learning Framework units, has been operated on a theoretical basis for the last six months with a representative number of programmes across the college. As from April 1993 these programmes have operated and evaluated an achievement-based model of resourcing.

The recognition by the FEFC that any funding mechanism should take into account the nature of learning processes in further education and the subsequent breakdown into the three elements – entry, being 'on programme', exit – was welcomed. A number of units have already been drafted for the Learning Framework which coincide with the elements described in *Funding Learning.* These include units for information and advice; initial assessment; action planning; induction; reviewing; opportunity awareness and exit/progression.

The achievement-based resourcing pilot, although theoretical, has clearly demonstrated the potential advantages to be had from adopting an alternative method of funding, not only from the perspective of the college manager who is responsible for resources, but also from the perspective of the learner/curriculum manager who is intent on maximising achievement.

Case Study 3: **CROYDON COLLEGE**

INTRODUCTION

The present Croydon College was founded in 1974 by merger of the former Technical College and the College of Art, which shared the same campus in the town centre. Since then the college has gained two additional sites and now has over 13,000 students attending on full-time, sandwich, block-release, day and/or evening or drop-in basis.

The case study is based on discussions with Liz Stopani, Director of College Marketing and Organisational Development. Its aim is to provide an overview of how the college is responding to community needs and to illustrate this by outlining some specific initiatives and achievements. The emphasis is on overall response to customer needs, rather than those of a particular group. However, the approaches the college has adopted are calculated to improve opportunities for adults and, in some cases, are specifically directed toward this.

COMMUNITY AND CUSTOMER FOCUS

Croydon College seeks to respond to local community needs while maintaining a strong focus on the individual student. Croydon is the largest commercial centre south-east of London and the college takes advantage of this by working closely with the local authority's Economic Development Unit, and in consortia with local firms and other organisations. In 1989 it began to focus strategically on 'the customer', and established a range of customer services which it continues to develop. These now include:

- assessment of prior learning and achievement
- information and guidance services
- accommodation help
- counselling services
- student welfare adviser
- learner and learning support centres and services
- information technology support
- work-based assessment
- advice on design and delivery of training plans.

POLICIES FOR ACCESS AND QUALITY OF PROVISION

The college has a strong equal opportunities policy both as an employer and as a service organisation. In opposing discrimination on grounds of gender, ethnic origin, age or disability it calls for positive action to promote equal opportunities for all these groups. The college's quality assurance system looks for evidence of this through regular review and evaluation of provision. This is in the context of the student/customer profile which, for the college as a whole, currently shows:

Gender: males 50.6 per cent, females 49.4 per cent

Age: 59 per cent over 18, 43 per cent over 21

Ethnic origin: 38 per cent non-white/European.

Access for adults is promoted by the college's role as a gateway centre for the Open College, with a wide variety of available OCN programmes. There is also a college commitment to developing open learning approaches within all courses and programmes, since it has been found that material which can be used in a flexible manner suits women returners and single parents in particular. For similar reasons most college courses have now been subdivided into short 'units' so that students can select those relevant to their needs.

There is an Access and Equal Opportunities Focus Group which includes representatives of technical, support and academic staff. Its remit is to identify any barriers to access faced by anyone wishing to study at the college, already studying there, and/or wishing to progress within the college. The group has produced a college AIDS policy. It has also designed, administered and analysed an equal opportunities questionnaire given to representative samples of staff and students. Findings have resulted in two sets of policy proposals – for staff and for students – to the college's Policy Planning and Strategy Group.

The quality assurance system plays a crucial role in the implementation of equal opportunities policies. Each course or programme team produces an annual programme review/evaluation report and action plan which is considered by the Quality Assurance sub-committee (AQA) and forms the basis of discussions between programme teams and quality staff. The Director of Quality chairs a Quality Focus Group and is also a member of the Access and Equal Opportunities Focus Group. As a result of this developments in the two areas have been closely linked, and the Quality Focus Group has produced statements on a series of student entitlements which are checked through the quality system under the following headings:

- guidance and tutorial support
- learner involvement in their learning process
- access to a variety of teaching methods
- assessment
- recording achievement
- learner involvement in (course) monitoring, evaluation and review.

CUSTOMER AND ADMINISTRATION SERVICES

There is a large and friendly 'customer and administration services' unit: 'It is the intention of the college that the services offered should be a seamless garment for the customer irrespective of whose management the service might fall under'. Security is unobtrusive and in this carpeted, plant-filled area students are offered:

- guidance and help on loans
- admission information and advice
- accreditation of prior learning and achievement
- examinations information, advice and records
- arrangements for assessment, including workplace assessment (three new members of staff have been appointed, each with responsibility for aspects of work placement, work-based learning and assessment)
- general college information.

The easily accessible College Information Centre (CIC) is the focus for anyone who is interested in what they can do at the college. It is open from 8.30am–8.30pm Monday to Thursday and 8.30am–5.00pm on Fridays. During the 1991/92 academic year CIC dealt with 38,700 face-to-face, telephone or written enquiries about education and training available at the college. While it carries promotional material for all college programmes and services, it may also refer clients to other providers and seeks to maintain effective networks with them; for example the following, several of which have a location within the college's customer services area:

- Croydon adult guidance and advice centre
- various counselling services, and community relations organisations
- CETS (Continuing Education and Training Service)
- the local Training and Enterprise Council (SOLOTEC)
- the Employment service
- local schools
- local and national agencies such as Citizens' Advice Bureau, Relate, etc.

EXTERNAL LINKS IN ADULT WORK

A current priority is to strengthen links between local adult education services and FE, especially for credit accumulation and transfer (CAT). Although there is much national work on CAT in both FE and HE, the adult to FE potential is as yet little explored outside Open College Networks. A key project is to review a 'Link Programme' run as a result of liaison between Croydon Continuing Education and Training Service (adult education) and Croydon

College. This has focused on a client group with qualifications from other countries, e.g. as doctors or lawyers, but needing help with English language and assistance on how to become recognised in this country. It seeks to bring people to the point where they can move into college programmes and achieve credit, and to identify barriers to this.

Review findings will impact on the college at a strategic level: 'where is the language support policy – we do not have strong enough language support throughout the college' (Liz Stopani). They will also mean looking at barriers in curriculum design and delivery, entry and admissions, and related administrative procedures.

Two further projects link with the college's CAT initiative and with improving adult access. An audit of common units is in progress in a newly-formed college school of studies which includes Hair and Beauty, Catering, Leisure, Travel and Tourism, with the aim of seeing how much credit accumulation and transfer can be encouraged. The other project is concerned with progression from Intermediate to Advanced GNVQs, which is being looked at jointly with a Sixth Form College partner. The Sixth Form College is seeking to increase its adult client group and sees Croydon College as the link institution for progression to the next level.

In a wider context the college is co-ordinating a SOLOTEC (South London TEC) project involving seven colleges and three adult education providers. SOLOTEC has agreed to retain a proportion of its WRFE funding to support a staff development programme related to credit accumulation and transfer for the providers involved:

All the work of the providers will be geared to supporting the implementation of credit accumulation and transfer, and will focus specifically on strengthening the relationship between adult education providers and their FE partners.

CURRICULUM STRATEGIES TO IMPLEMENT ACCESS POLICIES

A specific request from a course team recently led college management to conduct a thorough investigation of the implications of increasing the college's opening times – the team wanted to promote a 'two evenings plus Saturday' programme in Fashion in order to attract more adults. Issues included the availability of college facilities and services for students: when is the library open and fully operational; refectory; childcare; counsellors; open learning facilities, etc.? This was seen as an opportunity to test out the reality of Croydon College's claims to offer, for example, open access, flexible delivery, a range of facilities and services to meet customer needs. Again, needs for further development are being identified as a result. The college has also recently completed an evaluation of its GNVQ programmes which, amongst other findings, identified a potential for growth in its adult market: 'we will lose customers if we do not provide what they need' (from the evaluation report).

Following FEFC emphasis on the role of APL, the college is now revisiting its policy in this area. In particular it is looking at the need to have systems and structures that deal with APL both as an integral part of curriculum delivery in all programmes, and as a stand-alone service for candidates who may be otherwise 'external' to the college. There is a dedicated APL centre which focuses notably on certain NVQ areas such as Business, Care, Hairdressing and Beauty, Catering and Management. Currently targeted are Child Care and Development programmes, and plans have been agreed with Croydon Social Services Department to use APL for child-minders looking towards a level 2 NVQ.

Liz Stopani feels that APL has made many colleges and staff think much more carefully about programme design and delivery:

> It is not a fringe activity but part of a holistic approach to programme delivery and student support. Not all qualifications are at present constructed to allow partial credit, though, in some cases, credit gained from a qualification or part qualification can go towards meeting requirements for another award. One vital aspect of the APL process is that it encourages the individual to reflect on past experiences and acknowledge learning achievement, and so enhances self-esteem and self-confidence. It has also led to greater awareness of access, credit and other needs of mature students.

SOME ADULT ACHIEVEMENTS

Noticeboard, the college internal magazine, recently included the following item:

> Once again Croydon College has triumphed. This time it is Ms Gillian Stringer, a mature student on the Cert Ed course who has proved a winner. Gillian, who lives in West Croydon, is herself profoundly deaf and teaches sign language at several Adult Education Institutes under the auspices of CETS. She was nominated by the college because of her exceptional qualities in overcoming her learning difficulties and has been selected as one of the regional winners of the 1994 Outstanding Adult Learners Awards.

The judging panel consists of members of NIACE in collaboration with Carlton Television, and awards are presented by LASER (London and South East Regional Advisory Council).

One of the college's centres has, in its portfolio of provision, degree access programmes for adults:

An adult lounge has evolved – a space gradually transformed to include easy chairs, coffee machine, plants and music for varying tastes. As often happens it started with one member of staff identifying the need and, having an office in that area, beginning to reclaim the space. A recent SPOC (student perception of college) survey for adults showed their appreciation of a dedicated social area where it exists and the desire for one where it doesn't.

An NNEB (nursery nursing) programme for mature students is now offered on an outreach basis through consortium arrangements. Caring is seen as a growth area which, at the same time, is subject to continuous change stemming from demography, qualification structures and national policies. Development both within and outside the college is continually monitored, and action is taken to ensure that a wide range of progression routes is provided and keeps pace with changing needs.

Much remains to be done. There is at present a creche on only one of the college's sites, so that access for single parents is still too limited. 'Flexible' delivery should not mean leaving students to cope by themselves with computers. Corporate objectives include:

- to provide equality of opportunity through the institution, seeking to remove progressively any barrier to learning which may exist, and to recognise that each student and member of staff is a valued member of the college
- to seek to provide a high level of support and access for under-represented groups of students
- to use the full calendar year to provide college activities, and to extend the opening hours of the library and learning centres.

We often forget in FE that so many opportunities exist for us to reach adults – all of us in FE should remember that we are full-time ambassadors of education and training wherever we go and with everyone we meet. FE is still the least understood area of education – the public know about schools and universities but colleges need to check out their image, do a reality check. Do adults in your area just think of college as being the 'Tech' for young plumbers, not the place to go for careers or life planning advice?

Case Study 4: ST HELENS COMMUNITY COLLEGE

BACKGROUND

St Helens is a large college with a wide range of vocational and other programmes offered from five sites. The intake of full-time students at 16-plus is growing steadily, as is the number of adults attending full-time or by other modes. This can be put down to a variety of factors, among which are:

- a policy to create an 'open access' college, backed by strategies to ensure that this is achieved and linked with development of modular programmes
- energetic marketing and response to local community needs
- an approach to change that is both proactive and pragmatic, with an emphasis on realistic targets, action and concrete achievement
- management structures and college services that support continuing change and development.

Programmes

Provision is comprehensive, ranging from special needs programmes to HNDs and degrees. While GCSEs, A-levels and HE Access are offered, the college's vocational provision is particularly strong:

- as partner with over a dozen local schools in the St Helens Vocational Education Consortium the college provides link programmes for 14–16-year-old students sampling up to 15 vocational areas at eight different sites, and achieving 'VEC' credits that guarantee a place on college programmes; future plans include credit for NVQ units
- the college is a YT Managing Agent and students may choose at entry whether to join YT or full-time programmes
- there are over 50 NVQ programmes spanning levels 1–5 and including: Floristry and Horticulture; Business, Accounting and Management; Catering and Hairdressing; Retail and Wholesale; Construction and related (eight areas) and Engineering; Social Care and Training
- as a 'Phase 1' GNVQ centre for all five initial sectors St Helens has since added new sectors together with level 1 GNVQs; it also sees an adult market and plans to offer part-time GNVQ programmes (current full-time programmes include adults)
- the college is an active member of Merseyside Open College Federation, with several Access to FE and Access to HE programmes
- FE Access and other vocational provision for adults is considered in more detail in the final section of the case study.

82

Organisational structure

Previously the college had a faculty structure with only five people (Principal, two VPs, Personnel and Finance Directors) with clear cross-college functions. Since January 1992 Heads of School report in most cases to the Principal (renamed Chief Executive), who works with a directorate of seven. This includes Vice and Assistant Principals and its members respectively direct Quality and Curriculum (Q&C), Marketing, Planning, Finance, Personnel, Estates, and a major outlying campus.

Like her colleagues, Jackie Fisher, the Q&C Director, has no line responsibility for Schools of Study. However, she heads a range of central services and controls substantial funds that are 'top-sliced' from School budgets to provide for remission, staff development for curriculum change, resources for learning materials and other activities specifically approved by Q&C. She is assisted by five functional managers, including the Head of Curriculum, to whom report the Co-ordinator of Adult Programmes, the Core Skills Co-ordinator and six other staff with cross-college curriculum development roles. Other managers within the directorate include Student Services (pre-entry and ongoing student advice and guidance), Quality, Assessment and Learning Support and Learning Resources.

The newly created Marketing Unit has seven full-time professional staff including its Director. It is currently reviewing and developing the college's marketing strategy but is able to build from a strong base which includes, for example:

- College Corner, a chatty and informative weekly column in the local paper produced by the college Publicity Officer and supplemented on occasion by a pull-out section giving full details of college programmes and opportunities
- previous outreach work and a wide range of open days and other events at various locations
- detailed market intelligence gathered in recent years both by staff and by research students working at the college
- complementary work by Student Services, which gives information, advice and guidance to current and prospective students through the year.

ACCESS, DELIVERY AND SUPPORT

The college has two main and complementary curriculum strategies designed to promote open access to learning programmes and successful student achievement. While their purpose is to benefit all students they also offer radically improved opportunities for adults, especially when linked with initiatives outlined in the last section of this case study. They are:

- college-wide implementation of a policy of 'modularisation' underpinned by quality criteria and linked with flexibility of provision
- strong development of services and other initiatives to support students at entry; during; and at end of programmes, coupled with institution of a College Learning Policy to inform programme design and delivery.

Modularisation

St Helens has set up a modular framework which allows access throughout the year and promotes credit accumulation. Modules are based primarily on units of credit towards qualifications (e.g. BTEC, NVQs, GNVQs) although modules common to more than one programme are encouraged.

All modular programmes are divided into learning blocks of six (FE programmes) or 12 weeks (HE programmes) and the timing of blocks is common across the college. Students can thus enter a programme at the start of any block and take one or more modules either from a single programme or, where attendance time allows, from more than one programme. Depending on student numbers a module may be offered in one or more blocks through the year; for example, most HND Business and Finance modules are offered in all three blocks.

The framework already applies to a range of vocational programmes including some HNDs and NVQs, and all GNVQs. The number of units taken in each block may vary, e.g.: full-time students on the Business HND take three modules per 12–week block while, for GNVQ levels 2 and 3, mandatory and/or option units are generally taken at the rate of one per six-week block. Maximum 'supervised learning time' for an FE module is 15 hours per week (but may be much less than this) while 'delivery time' for an HE module is a maximum four hours per week. FE students may thus be limited to one module per block, though (for example) GNVQ students may also take a GNVQ 'Additional' unit, NVQ unit or, in future, A/AS-level module.

A 40-page *Staff Handbook on Modularisation* explains the framework and gives guidance on implementation. It includes detailed sections on:

- teaching and learning methods, with an emphasis on the need to shift the balance between 'taught' and learning/support sessions
- access to programmes at points during the year, and flexible delivery methods that allow for individually-negotiated timetables
- tutorial systems to provide regular support, action planning and review, and link in with the college's central learner support services

- support at entry and exit, including effective induction, review of achievement, and progression to other modules
- relevant qualifications, the learner's opportunity to obtain these and progression to another FE/HE programme
- curriculum-led staff development: changing roles of programme teams/ tutors/managers, the need for new types of skill, and the monitoring and supporting role of the Q&C Directorate.

In defining the characteristics of a module, the *Staff Handbook* also shows the criteria which will be progressively applied in college validation and approval of modules and modular programmes. These provide that a module should:

- be stated in learning outcomes
- identify access requirements and progression opportunities
- provide learning and assessment by a range of methods
- not be time-constrained for the learner but have a notional time allocation for the lecturer.

It is also made clear that there should be an increasing move to flexible delivery that includes accreditation of prior achievement, assessment on demand, and varied learning opportunities to suit individual needs and study/attendance modes.

Individual student support

Most centrally-provided student support services and initiatives at St Helens come under the Q&C Directorate. The list of activities outlined below includes two that are shared (Admissions and 'Study Plus'). It is not exhaustive but shows some of the practical steps the college has taken to focus on the needs of individual students and potential clients. These are seen as even more crucial with the introduction of modular provision.

Central Admissions: An administrative function outside the Q&C Directorate which deals with admissions and registrations at any time of the year.

Student Services Units: Before registering for a programme/module students are likely first to have visited a Student Services Unit. These are open on college sites throughout the week and the college year to potential and current students. They offer advice, guidance and counselling on programmes/qualifications, learning needs/opportunities, career requirements, etc., and assist with initial action planning.

Options Centre: A college-LEA-TEC partnership was then to set up to run an 'Options Centre' at the main college sites. It provides educational guidance for adults (though adults may also use Student Services) and access to an APL service.

Study Plus Scheme: All full-time students at the college whether school leavers or adults receive a 'Study Plus' package that includes free travel, a book voucher, and a stationery pack. Similar help may be given to non-employed adults not registered as unemployed (e.g. women returners). The service is financed from the college budget and, to facilitate this, the college has a member of staff employed full time to identify potential sources of outside funding.

Learning Support Centre: Centres at several sites provide learning support for individual students, who attend either of their own volition or on referral by tutors. Support may include diagnostic assessment, help with learning problems including numeracy and literacy, or with the development of portfolios. The Centre is also developing an independent assessment service to provide APL and assessment on demand.

Open Learning: Cross-college approaches to open learning are currently being developed. While self-study materials have been produced for a range of modules/programmes, they have so far been used mainly for normal programme delivery rather than separate open learning provision.

Learning Policy: There is a formally defined College Learning Policy with four key elements: (1) Flexible Individualised Learning including individual action planning and a variety of learning pathways; (2) Modularisation (see above); (3) Flexible Assessment including APL, assessment on demand, workplace assessment, core skills; (4) Student Care, focused on the learner's needs and personal programme at admission, entry to programme, during the programme, at end/progression. Implementation of the policy is monitored by the Q&C Directorate.

PROVISION FOR ADULTS

St Helens has, like most FE colleges, a majority of students (currently 76 per cent) over 19. It has also had for some time a range of full- and part-time programmes for adults, including vocational preparation and FE Access courses at various levels offered under the aegis of the Merseyside Open College Federation. These programmes were generally quite separate from the college's 'mainstream' provision. In 1990, after the appointment of a new principal, the college adopted a policy to increase adult participation in vocational programmes, especially for women. This had immediate and radical results, which are outlined below.

New opportunities for adults

It was decided in 1990 to put a bid to the European Social Fund under Objectives 3 (training/retraining long-term unemployed over-25s) and 4 (basic and higher skills training for under-25s). The project was headed by Geraldine Miles (now Head of Curriculum) whose background was vocational programmes, working with Marianne McCracken (now Access to FE Manager), who had a background in adult education. As well as ensuring that hitherto separate experience of vocational programmes and of teaching adults was brought together, this became the college's first major exercise in centralised curriculum development:

- labour market research was carried out, skills shortages identified and unemployment figures collected
- a one-day workshop was held for all Heads of School and leaders of main programme areas/divisions
- Heads of School were asked to put forward ideas for vocational programmes that could be offered to adults, and to make commitments
- a wide range of programmes was put forward, many of them quite new, and these were organised into a successful bid
- implementing the proposals brought over 400 new/additional adult students into the college on full-time programmes, supported by means of a travel pass, fee remission and free meals
- newly developed courses within the programme include: New Opportunities for Adults in Travel and Tourism, and Women into Media
- some courses start in September, others in January or April, while a number take entrants at fixed points or on a roll-on-off basis
- attendance is normally 15–21 hours a week (ensuring no loss of Benefits) and is, where possible, arranged to fit in with adult commitments (e.g. 9.30am–3.00pm over three-and-a-half days)
- some programmes are purely for adults and women returners, while others are offered on an 'in-fill' basis.

Many staff found themselves 'in at the deep end' in teaching adults for the first time, especially in having to deal with problems outside learning – e.g. finance, family and personal problems. A programme of staff development was carried out and much learning came from working with adults and sharing experience with other staff. Many staff acquired new skills and attitudes, with the result that the college became far better equipped to offer an effective service to adult clients.

Building on the experience and success of the New Opportunities project, it was decided that the college's short Access provision should be restructured; this has now been done, is in place and developing. The new structure involves in-depth pre-course guidance to determine the area of interest and adults then attend college 15 hours a week for one term. Core modules are offered in 'broad' vocational areas such as service industries, technology.

Individuals may also choose from a range of 'option' modules which include Literacy, Numeracy, IT, Assertiveness, Study Skills, Counselling Skills.

This approach allows adults to sort out their own level, any personal and practical problems that may affect their return to study, and to explore their chosen vocational area fully before making a final commitment. On-course guidance is built in to ensure that adults progress to the best course for them at the right level. Drop-out rates amongst adult returners are expected to decrease markedly as a result. The Access to FE programme continues to expand, with an intake of students every 12 weeks.

Adult markets

The college carries out a significant amount of marketing activity directed specifically at adults. Previous outreach work in the community proved uneconomic and perhaps unnecessary, since current activity brings a more than satisfactory response. This includes:

- separate publicity, leaflets, many press releases and items in local newspapers
- posters and information at Adult Education Centres
- a physical college presence in Job Centres
- discussions with firms planning redundancies, leading to the offer of specific services
- special events, including activities during Adult Learners' Week.

It is felt that there are other untapped markets, and the college is still working to fill gaps in its provision. A recently advertised course for women returners to train in Information Technology brought an overwhelming response. Systematic destination surveys have been carried out for students who entered the college at 16-plus and it is now planned, with the help of a research student, to extend this to adults who come onto college programmes.

Full implementation of learning and modularisation policies should further increase adult participation and the college is in no doubt that this is needed. For example, in many colleges work in Construction is under threat and in some has been discontinued; at St Helens very substantial work has been maintained in this area but would not have been viable without large numbers of adult students.

Case Study 5: CUMBRIA COLLEGE OF ART AND DESIGN (CCAD)

BACKGROUND: A PROCESS OF RADICAL CHANGE

CCAD is a 'one department college' with some 30 full-time teaching staff and had, until fairly recently, an almost wholly full-time clientele mainly doing BTEC National or Higher National courses. From this base it embarked on a process of systematic and radical development which is likely to continue. Features of this include :

- ongoing review of programmes and markets, resource use and delivery methods, college structure and staff roles
- a continuing shift towards HE programmes – five vocational degrees started from September 1993
- parallel franchising of BTEC First and year 1 National (GNVQ levels 2/3 from September 1993) to schools and FE colleges county-wide, and of specific HNDs to certain colleges on a national basis
- extending provision to new areas such as performing arts, media studies, heritage and environment studies, tourism, etc.
- sharp and sustained increase in student numbers without increased teaching staff – in 1993/4 there were 20 per cent more full-time students than in 1992/3, almost twice as many as in 1988, and growth continues
- wholly unit-based provision since 1989/90, based at that time on BTEC awards but now applied GNVQ and degree programmes.

Impetus for change

The process began in 1987 when the senior management team (Principal, Vice-Principal, Director of Studies, Director of Resources) carried out a review of the college in the context of future changes such as ERA and NCVQ:

We started looking at the products available from the college, i.e. our courses of study; the functions of the college and the functional roles of people employed within the college. Tried to compare ourselves with a business, looked at the functional areas of businesses and worked out what we should be doing that we were either ignoring completely, or doing badly. (Charles Mitchell, Director of Studies.)

It was found that almost all the work of management, teaching and other staff was focused on current products, and that this was reflected in college structures. Courses ran as separate units with team leaders in charge of budgets, and staff with cross-college roles were often marginalised. Product development and marketing functions existed only as time and money 'stolen' from teaching and from course budgets. Courses were linear, with little choice of options or learning style:

> We didn't particularly like the way we were offering our courses of study, and the lack of flexibility we had in offering those courses. It was fine if somebody turned up in September and had nothing better to do for the next two years – but we weren't catering for somebody who wanted to start a specific part of a course and wanted to start in February or somebody who, for perfectly valid reasons, wanted a hybrid course that drew from two or more of our validated courses. (Charles Mitchell, Director of Studies.)

Aims and strategy

Delivery structure was seen as the key to change and a framework was devised to transform this. Aims were to provide for personal learning programmes, more flexible delivery and a wider range and choice of provision. It was decided to:

- revise management roles to strengthen marketing and product development
- define teaching staff roles by functional areas based on managing the learning process
- set in motion a staged plan to make all current provision modular, bring in new modular products and market more widely
- develop flexible delivery methods such as open and resource-based learning
- set up a college assessment framework which would support more open access and flexible delivery.

NEW COLLEGE STRUCTURE AND STAFF ROLES

During 1988/89 a staff skills audit ('bit similar to a user-friendly appraisal scheme') was carried through to define roles within the new delivery framework. Staff were each interviewed and asked their views on the role and direction of the college, their own place in this and their future interests. This led to all staff having one or more of three distinct functional roles:

Programmers (4)	Personal Guidance Tutors (PGTs) (11)	Subject Specialists (20+)
Managing a portfolio of programmes (wider role than old course leaders)	Negotiating individual student programmes and co-ordinating progress	Programme delivery: designing learning activities and carrying out assessment
Developing new programmes	Counselling, tutorial support, careers guidance	Managing and supervising workshops and studios
Programme design and validation	Feedback on programme delivery	Budget control for area of work
Programme scheduling and timetabling	Co-ordinating student assessments and student records	Developing industry-linked projects and assessment
Quality assurance: moderator links, course review, monitoring and evaluation	Liaison with Subject Specialists on student progress	Contracting, briefing and supervising outside (e.g. industry) specialists
INSET needs for programme delivery	Admissions and initial guidance, including diagnosis and APL	Quality control and standards of work

The new structure was brought in during 1989 after being worked through and agreed in a series of staff conference days. At the time Director of Studies Charles Mitchell saw the whole exercise as a learning process in which objectives would be refined and details changed as experience grew – 'we have a long way to go yet but we're learning all the time'. Now the structure remains but with shifts of emphasis reflected in altered role titles.

Programme Leaders ('Programmers') Have been able, because of shifts in administrative and other functions, to focus very strongly on developing new programmes – leading to radical change in the college's overall portfolio over the past four years.

Unit Tutors ('Subject Specialists') Have acquired a more central role because of the focus on unit-based delivery – they carry out much of the tutorial guidance originally allocated to 'PGTs'.

Academic Counsellors ('PGTs') In a recent independent evaluation of the Academic Counselling system 'ACs' were seen to play a key role in the unit based delivery system. Most valued elements of the role were:

- help with student development of learning skills, self-assessment and action planning

91

- two-way communication on assessment – evidence on student achievement for Assessment Boards, and feedback from programme teams/unit tutors to students
- neutrality/independence, ensuring both natural justice and rigour in assessment – jealously guarded by staff and students alike
- crucial contribution to quality assurance in providing critical feedback on unit delivery and learning programmes.
  Important issues arising from the evaluation included:
- dramatic increase in Academic Counsellor workload with fuller recognition of the role – tendency of some unit tutors to 'offload' less palatable duties to Academic Counsellors
- linked problem of Academic Counsellor overload with administrative duties and information – need to clarify division of functions between programme teams/Academic Counsellors/administrative staff, review costs/value for money, and balance against management information system priorities
- problems of balancing neutral role on assessment with student support – and advocacy where necessary
- issues of student ownership of achievement, openness of information on and ownership of assessment – need for clearer practice guidelines.

ACCESS AND DELIVERY

Unit-based provision

All college provision has for some time been delivered and assessed on a unit or 'modular' basis – this applies equally to level 3 BTEC/GNVQs, HNDs, degrees and non-vocational provision for adults. The original purpose was to increase flexibility so that students could enter at different points of the year to access individual units, agreed combinations or a whole programme/qualification. In the event this purpose has not yet been achieved:

- student demand for full-time programmes at the college has increased, and has supported continued focus on these rather than on separate access to individual units
- while attempts have been made to accommodate students entering during the year and/or wanting specific units, numbers have been relatively small and there have been problems: some adults on individual programmes have dropped out either because units failed to 'stand alone' or because materials and support systems did not meet their needs

92

- enquiries suggest a real need for flexible provision but enquirers may be turned away either because a suitable programme cannot be designed or because it is felt that current delivery systems cannot offer enough support
- there have been notable successes: for example, a request for training in animation techniques was received from an Italian college – shortly afterwards two clients flew over for a three-week programme and completed two units.

The lesson that unit-based or 'modular' provision does not in itself increase flexibility is seen as important and has emphasised the need for other approaches to improved access which are outlined below. On the positive side the early experience of developing unit-based provision has proved a valuable learning exercise and has, for example, led to a policy of common units between degree programmes (not applied to earlier BTEC unit-based programmes). This serves to rationalise resources but also helps shift the focus of delivery away from purely course-based provision.

Resource-based delivery

An increasing number of units are now delivered entirely through 'resource-based' learning whereby students access workshops at any time, provided space allows, pursue a programme of activities and obtain tutor advice as needed. This has been given high priority, is managed by four senior members of the teaching staff and enables better use of scarce staff resources and overall provision for more students. However, it is limited to areas of work which depend on practice and do not involve direct teaching, and/or where learner packs have been developed. These facilities are at present used only for full-time programmes but also offer a basis for future access by students attending individually by a variety of modes.

Shifts in attendance mode

The college has sought to provide for a wider range of attendance modes and to target new client groups, including adults. This remains an important objective although achievement has so far been limited, and most programmes and students still tend to be treated as full-time. However, providing for greatly increased student numbers with strictly limited resources has led to subtle changes in attendance mode and to a blurring in practice of 'full-time' and 'part-time':

- pressure on resources is such that a 'shift' system is used for some full-time groups, one being in college for the first half of the week and another the second half (perhaps including some Saturday work), with both groups present mid-week for joint lectures

- to support this, formal staff-student contact time on full-time programmes has been reduced steadily from an original 24 hours to 18 hours a week in 1993/94 and a proposed 15 hours in 1994/95
- although there has been substantial investment in increased study and workshop space this is not always sufficient and, where appropriate, tutors may agree with individual students that they can work at home for certain sessions
- while there may questions about what is meant by 'attendance' on a 'full-time programme' for funding purposes, considerable flexibility is possible in practice and some 'full-time' students are effectively attending part-time on a basis that may vary from week to week.

Currently the college is focusing on establishing its new degree courses in 'full-time' mode and on providing effective programmes for increased numbers of students. However, it plans to introduce more systematic and flexible part-time provision from 1995.

Work-based learning and assessment

CCAD vocational programmes are centred on work-based assignments and projects that involve close links with companies. A group of students may spend a day with, for example, a large advertising agent to work out a design brief for a given purpose. If a firm is interested in a design produced in this way, CCAD may pay development costs to realise it to commercial standards and students will carry out the work involved. Overall, the college recoups costs from designs sold to firms through this process – a Clydesdale Bank credit card in current use was, for example, designed by CCAD students.

The college has found the slow development of NVQs in the Design area somewhat frustrating. It recognises that in due course it will need to develop more work-based assessment and sees NVQs as an opportunity to meet the needs of more adult students.

Adult students

Although provision is still mainly full-time, the proportion of students over 21 on some programmes is as much as 50 per cent and, in one case, average age is over 30. There is also a diagnostic programme offered up to three times a year and largely attended by adults. This enables students to try out and be assessed in a range of Art and Design activities, to develop a variety of skills and, where appropriate, to progress to a suitable programme at BTEC National/GNVQ 3, HND or degree level. NVQs should eventually provide an additional option, as well as an opportunity to develop more systematic approaches to APL.

While the supply of full-time students at 16-plus and 18-plus from schools and franchised FE colleges is still growing for CCAD, it is recognised that this will not necessarily continue indefinitely. At the same time the college believes there is both a market and a community need for more adult provision. It intends to continue to work towards this, feels it has established a strong base for developing more flexible provision and plans, in particular, to review this alongside the introduction of part-time programmes in 1995.